Why won't my child listen?

Why won't my child listen?

Myra Grisdale & Janet Cater
with Michael Morton-Evans

SIMON & SCHUSTER
AUSTRALIA

First published in Australia in 2005 by
Simon & Schuster (Australia) Pty Limited
Suite 2, Lower Ground Floor
14–16 Suakin Street, Pymble NSW 2073

A Viacom Company
Sydney New York London Toronto Singapore

Visit our website at www.simonsaysaustralia.com

Cataloguing-in-Publication data:

Cater, Janet.
    Why won't my child listen ?
    Includes index.
    ISBN 0 7318 1230 1.
    1. Child development.   2. Parenting.   3. Child rearing.   I.
    Grisdale Myra.   II. Morton-Evans, Michael.   III. Title.
649.1

Extract from *This Be the Verse* by Philip Larkin reprinted with
the kind permission of Faber and Faber Ltd

Cover design by Christabella Designs
Cover illustration by Jody Pratt, Hot Trash Studios
Internal illustration by Ian Faulkner
Typeset in 12 on 16pt Perpetua by Kirby Jones
Printed in Australia by Griffin Press

10 9 8 7 6 5 4 3 2

contents

ACKNOWLEDGMENTS

A particular thanks to Paula Cole, mother of four children under nine, who knows what it's like and patiently read through the early drafts to test out some of our theories. Thanks also to Jacquie Brown at Simon & Schuster, whose task it was to edit this book. We couldn't have asked for a better editor, especially given the fact that it was her first job back from maternity leave following the birth of her first child!

introduction

U ntil relatively recently the natural order of things, as defined by Darwin at least, was that the older generation took on the responsibility of teaching the young. They did this because they knew about life, and it was considered their responsibility to pass on their knowledge to the next generation.

Then everything changed. Probably the single most revolutionary factor in this change was the rapid advance of technology in the latter half of the 20th century, coupled with the growth of educational availability and the accessibility of knowledge. Possibly for the first time in the history of humankind, children were in a position to teach their parents a thing or two.

This change in teaching patterns was recorded first in 1952, interestingly not among humans, but among monkeys. Since the 1920s scientists had been studying the habits of a colony of *Macaca fuscata*, a species of monkey that lives in Japan. These monkeys normally eat a variety of buds, leaves, fruits and the bark of over 100 types of plant. Their pattern of eating had been taught to them by their mothers who, in turn, had learned from their mothers.

As part of an experiment, the scientists started giving the monkeys raw sweet potatoes covered with sand to eat, a situation alien to the monkeys. For a time this perplexed the monkeys — until one day in 1952 when a young female hit on a solution to the problem. She took her potato to a nearby stream and began washing the sand off it. The pleased youngster then taught this trick to her mother, thereby reversing the age-old pattern of instruction. She also taught her playmates, who taught their families. Slowly the number of monkeys washing their potatoes grew, until, in 1958, there was a startling explosion in the number of monkeys using the technique.

Inexplicably, monkeys all over mainland Japan, and even on the outlying islands, began washing their food at the same time — an event that has become known as the Hundredth Monkey Effect. Translated to the human world, this creates considerable confusion (particularly among older parents) as to the exact nature of their roles.

Each successive generation has lived with its version of the 'generation gap', the void that seems to stretch between most parents and children. In the early years of the 21st century that gap is arguably the widest it has ever been.

What used to be a funny kindergarten joke has become a reality — two five-year-olds are talking; one says to the other, 'I found a contraceptive on our verandah the other day.' Replies the other, 'What's a verandah?'

Six-year-olds now play computer games better and faster than their parents. By the age of ten, most will know more about computer operating systems than their parents, and you can always tell when there isn't a teenager in the house — the timer on the video machine is blinking!

Given that the vast majority of parents have only one set of guidelines for bringing up their children, that is, the manner in which their parents brought them up, in this vastly changed age even the best parents may start to lose confidence in their ability. Unconfident parenting is often responsible for children being allowed to dominate a family, a situation that can force parents to fall back on authoritarian ways, which only leads to more rebellion and frustration in their children.

The continued rise in incidents of teenage suicide, anorexia, attention deficit disorder (ADD), depression and schizophrenia is worrying to say the least. For the past 20 years Myra Grisdale, a psychologist and child education professional, and Janet Cater, an early childhood and parenting specialist, have been working to find new approaches to parenting, as well as children's learning and behavioural issues, which might lead to a new generation of happy, confident and motivated parents with well-balanced, confident children.

The conclusion they have reached is quite simply this: If you understand your child from an early age and encourage them through the various techniques outlined in this book, then there is a greater chance that your child will become a happy and well-adjusted teenager and, hopefully, go on to become a well-balanced adult.

Of course, not every child is the same and therefore the results may vary. And there is no such thing as the perfect parent. On some days as parents we face new challenges and may feel a bit like a P-plate driver, while on others it's a straight drive up the highway. Some days are easier than others. We advise looking upon each day as a clean slate.

One of the main reasons why children don't listen to their parents is that they don't feel their parents listen to them, and, consequently, don't understand them. Some parents may have a tendency to 'nag' their child — another sure-fire way of causing a child to switch off. The techniques described in this book will enable parents to bridge that seemingly bottomless pit that is parent–child understanding. Naturally it's going to be easier if you can start using these techniques early in your child's life, but no matter what age your child is when you come to this book, you will find some invaluable advice which can make a profound difference at any age.

1

it all starts
with you

Without a doubt, having children can be one of life's most enriching experiences. There is an enormous feeling of satisfaction and joy in watching a child grow up and knowing that you, the parents, are responsible for helping turn a chrysalis into a butterfly.

But, at the same time, children can also be very hard work. They are a lifetime commitment. They can be expensive, both financially and emotionally. In short, they are the single biggest responsibility of your whole life. How you behave around your children will affect them enormously, though you may not always realise it.

> They fuck you up, your mum and dad.
> They may not mean to, but they do.
> They fill you with the faults they had
> And add some extra, just for you.[1]

So wrote British poet Philip Larkin, who was offered the job of poet laureate to the Queen of England but turned it down because he could not face the notoriety that went with the position. Some thought it a pity he refused. Based on this quote alone he might be able to teach the British Royal Family a thing or two!

So let's start by asking this question: why do you want a child? Clearly this is a question that requires a careful answer. Too many people tend to rush into parenthood for all the wrong reasons, and both their lives and that of their children are adversely affected. It is important to be aware of what you are letting yourself in for before you take the big step of parenthood, for everyone's sake.

"Why do you want a child? This question requires a careful answer."

OK, that's enough lecturing. But it is serious. Here's an outline of some of the important issues you need to consider before planning a child.

For a start, babies don't come with instruction manuals. Philip Larkin actually was dead right. The only training most of us have as parents comes from our own parents and how they brought us up. If they made a good job of it, then the odds are you'll make quite a good job of it, too. If they made a lot of mistakes along the way, it is more than likely you'll make the same mistakes if you don't ask for or receive any help.

If you do want to seek help, where do you start? There are so many parenting books on bookstore shelves, all offering a variety of techniques, not to mention all those well-meaning friends only too willing to impart their knowledge to you, however scanty. It is very easy to become confused very quickly.

So, you say, what's this then, if it isn't just another of those parenting books to confuse us further? Well, the difference with this book is that we are going to make *you* do the work. Our job is to act merely as a guide along the rocky path of parenthood. When all's said and done, it's you, the parents, who are going to have to make the final climb from base camp to the summit.

VALUES AND HOW THEY PLAY THEIR PART

The worst possible start any child can have in life is one where the parents cannot agree on anything. It is imperative that both parents have a clear idea of where they are heading when it comes to bringing up a child. Your principal role as a parent is to act as a role model. Some parents try to be their child's best friend — a nice idea, but the child will probably not be short of friends while growing up. However, they will generally only ever have one set of parents and the job of those parents is to *parent* them.

Parenting involves giving your child security — physical, emotional and intellectual — and providing a road map for them to follow, on what is becoming an increasingly difficult journey for young people.

Where better to start than with your own values? Values are a set of personal beliefs in which a person has an emotional investment (either for or against something). We all have them, and it is important when deciding whom you are going to marry and share children with to discover whether your intended partner has similar values to yours, or widely differing ones. A major difference in values is one of the most common causes of relationship breakdown, whether it be parent to parent or parent to child.

The fundamental importance of values in raising children is slowly being realised and implemented in schools around the world with a United Nations initiative called Living Values: An Educational Program. This innovative global education program offers a wide range of values activities and practical methods to educators, facilitators, parents and caregivers that enable children and young adults to explore and develop 12 universal values: unity, simplicity, responsibility, happiness, humility, honesty, respect, peace, love, tolerance, freedom and cooperation.

This program has so far been implemented in 74 countries at over 7000 schools. Reports from educators state that the program has enhanced both teacher–student and student–student relationships inside and outside the classroom, with an increase in positive behaviour such as cooperation, respect and motivation, and a decrease in aggressive behaviour.

We need, as parents, to get our message straight on these 12 basic values and then impart them to our children. Unless we have a set of values that basically agrees with those of our partners, giving clear messages to our children might be difficult. Children pick up on the things they hear their parents saying and tend to mix them up in their heads unless the message is very clear. As an example, some time ago we asked two ten-year-olds, Jack and Megan, how they thought they would decide on whom to marry. Out of the mouths of babes, as the saying goes, came these two telling responses:

> **Jack:** 'You've got to find somebody who likes the same sort of stuff as you. Like, if you're into sports, she should like it that you like sports, and she should keep the chips and dip coming.'
> **Megan:** 'No person really decides before they grow up who they're going to marry. God decides it long before and you get to find out later who you're stuck with.'

Well, Jack sort of got it right. Ideally you need to find somebody who thinks along the same lines as you do. Where he picked up the sexist message about the chips and dips is anyone's guess!

Let's examine in brief some of the bigger questions, from education and discipline through to religion and money.

What do you believe about education?

Many parents today believe that children must be given every advantage to learn and achieve high academic results in order to go to university and become the best doctor, lawyer or accountant in the land.

Is this necessarily right? We don't believe so. The best approach is to look at each child's uniqueness and gently steer them to where they can learn by discovery and interest and so blossom into happy, balanced adults. What may work educationally for one sibling may not work for another.

Many schools today push children really hard. Homework is doled out in large amounts to children as young as five or six. This is totally inappropriate and unnecessary. If your child has an unquenchable thirst for knowledge, then this education system may work, but in our experience many children wither and suffer under this system. For infant and primary school children, after-school time is for playing, running about and kicking balls. Otherwise it should be called 'more school' rather than 'after school'.

Children who are already struggling are given more work and parents then end up in a battlefield every afternoon nagging, bribing and cajoling their children to do homework, when they could be playing, or relaxing with you, building bonds and healthy relationships, which in turn fosters self-esteem. The key is to find a system that best suits your child, and that may not be one with an emphasis on high achievement and academic results. Education and learning is, of course, important, but it must not be at the expense of self-esteem and family relationships.

In short, we don't agree with the huge emphasis on homework today. Teachers say parents expect it while many parents tell us that teachers expect too much and it causes conflict in the home. Some feel they are constantly arguing with their child about homework. These issues and real concerns need to be communicated to teachers.

After sitting still and learning for the previous six or so hours, children need to be able to play and relax. A short time each day for infants and primary school children to reinforce learning is quite sufficient.

HOMEWORK TIPS

Given that most schools expect children to complete homework, here are some tips we hope will help you incorporate it with the least negative impact on the home, the family, the routine and relationships.

- Ensure your child has at least 30 to 60 minutes' relaxation or down time after school before commencing homework. Give active and physical children opportunities to run, climb or kick a ball.
- Use some Brain Gym movements before homework time to switch on the brain (see Chapter 4).
- Encourage your child to talk about their day.
- Encourage them to drink plenty of water.
- Ensure they have eaten a nutritious afternoon tea.
- Try to make homework fun — set up a special 'homework' place.
- Provide new pens or pencils just for homework.
- Provide a jazzy clock or timer so they know when homework time is over — this gives them some control.
- For children under ten, help and guide.
- Discuss the best time to do homework.
- Maintain communication with teachers regarding expectations.
- Find out whether the teacher would rather have everything completed or incomplete but correct and understood.
- Establish if your child prefers you to work alongside them, or look over the homework after it is completed.
- Avoid making homework a big deal. Don't threaten or bribe your child with rewards/withdrawal of privileges.

It is not uncommon for children to be pushed by their parents and teachers into areas in which they are not really suited. Learning may then cease to be interesting and stimulating and the child will switch off. Often this can lead to academic struggle, unhappiness and low self-esteem for the child and heartache for the parents. Some of these children will often come back to tertiary education later in life when they have discovered who they are and what they really want to do.

What do you believe about discipline?

There are parents who are harsh disciplinarians, and those who go to the other extreme and don't discipline their children at all. Both positions are equally harmful and unhelpful to the child.

Children need to push up against something to make sense of their world. They need to know that there are barriers designed for their safety and that, as parents, we are obliged to help them grow and make decisions about self-regulating their behaviour. This helps them to feel safe. Of course, human nature being what it is, they will rebel from time to time and try to break through these barriers. That's only normal. They are testing their boundaries and you'd worry if they didn't ever try. All you need is clear communication, positive language, unconditional love and and, above all, *consistency*.

"Children need to push up against something to make sense of their world."

When it comes to discipline, consistency is crucial. The worst thing you can do is confuse a child by changing the goal posts every five minutes during the game. Children need to know exactly where they stand at all times, and that you are serious — so don't say anything you aren't prepared to carry through.

What do you believe about manners?

How important are manners? In a civilised society, most of us believe that good manners are important. Let's face it, there's nothing more unpleasant than an ill-mannered person, particularly a child, and no doubt we've all known a few! A child will learn good manners principally through example, rather than being nagged and reprimanded. As parents, we should act as role models by being respectful to others, being present in conversation by stopping what we are doing, making eye contact when we speak to people, showing concern and consideration for others, and always saying 'please' and 'thank you'. With small children, life is usually a matter of 'monkey see, monkey do'. If you use four-letter words in front of a five-year-old, don't be surprised when they crop up in her conversations. If you make disparaging remarks about other people or ignore somebody when they are speaking to you, don't expect your child to behave any differently or listen to you when you try to change their behaviour. They are merely copying your example and you have a snowball's chance in hell of trying to explain that there is one set of rules for grown-ups and one for children.

What do you believe about diet?

This is a tricky one. People's dietary tastes are usually dictated by their upbringing and their financial status. It is no coincidence that some of the fattest people in the Western world are also the poorest. It is, nevertheless, a well-documented fact that for children to learn and grow they need to have a healthy diet. Foods high in sugar, artificial colouring and preservatives are detrimental to long-term health — many articles have been written about how these contribute to the growing incidence of obese children and infantile diabetes. There is also ample proof that these kinds of foods also play a part in the increasingly common childhood symptoms and behaviours categorised as attention deficit disorder, or ADD. Snack foods and lollies should therefore be kept to a minimum.

Again, parents can teach by example by only supplying wholesome foods at home, eating healthy food themselves and making healthy choices.

What do you believe about religion?

If you thought diet was tricky, this one's even trickier! More arguments and wars have been started around the world in the name of religion than practically any other subject. If both parents hold the same religious belief — or none at all — it is simpler to agree on how the children will be brought up. Two parents, however, harbouring different religious beliefs can cause untold problems for a child unless the matter has been discussed and agreed upon in advance. The combinations are many — Catholic married to Protestant, Christian married to agnostic, Muslim married to Hindu, and so on. If two parents practise different religions, it is important that each respects the other and that an agreement is reached as to how their children will receive religious instruction.

Parents who practise their religion and demonstrate their faith to their children teach through example rather than coercion. As children become more articulate, parents can encourage discussion and debate on other religious and spiritual beliefs. This will empower children to make informed choices for themselves as to the spiritual or religious path they would like to follow. Travelling to other countries, reading stories about different cultures and tasting and eating food from other countries all contribute to children finding their own opinions and beliefs.

There are the odd pitfalls in encouraging open discussion, however, as demonstrated by this true story that took place between Michael and Maria and their daughter Sasha. Sasha, aged seven, was chatting to her mum and dad about religion one evening at the dinner table:

Sasha: 'Does everyone believe in Jesus?'
Maria: 'No.'
Sasha: 'How does it work?'
Maria: 'He was important and we respect that tradition.'
Sasha: 'What do you believe?'
Maria: 'That he was an example of love, compassion and tolerance, and an important person, but I don't believe in the "Son of God" bit.'

Sasha: 'Do you believe the same as Mum, Dad?'

Michael: 'Pretty much.'

Sasha: 'Do you have to marry someone who believes the same as you?'

Maria: 'No, but it is often why people get together, because they believe the same thing — they connect on that level.'

Sasha: 'So what if they don't?'

Maria: 'It's OK, so long as you respect what someone believes, you don't necessarily have to think the same about everything. Dad and I have some different opinions. You don't have to believe what we do, you may decide to believe in Jesus. You can find your own way.'

There is a thoughtful pause.

Sasha: 'Tilly, my friend at school, and I are sisters. We are all God's children. Mrs Morrison, our scripture teacher, told us God is like our father and we are all sisters in God's family.'

Michael: 'No, we're not. Tilly's your friend.'

Sasha: 'I thought you just said we can all believe what we want to and you have to respect what I believe.'

Michael: 'Sorry … you're right!'

What do you believe about money?

The following statement was written over 2000 years ago in a letter:

Those who want to get rich fall into temptation and are caught in the trap of many foolish and harmful desires, which pull them down to ruin and destruction. For the love of money is a source of all kinds of evil.

Over the centuries this message that St Paul wrote to Timothy, a young Christian from Asia Minor, became corrupted into today's common saying 'Money is the root of all evil.' This may be a bit extreme, but many people do attach far greater importance to money than they do to some of the other less tangible, but possibly more important, things in life. How important is money in your life? Do you use it to bribe your children? ('If you're quiet for the next half-hour, I'll give you a dollar.') Do you use it in place of quality time? ('Here's fifteen dollars, you can go the cinema. Mum's a bit busy today.') Or to appease a guilty conscience? ('I'm sorry I didn't take you to the football like I promised yesterday. Here's ten dollars, go to the shops and buy yourself something nice to make up for it.')

Money has quite definite uses, but bribing your children or using it to appease a guilty conscience is not beneficial to anyone. Bribery only leads to demotivation and, in the end, your child will only do things if they are paid. Children need to grow up with a healthy attitude to money. They need to learn how to use it appropriately and how to save it. Again, your values concerning the use of money will serve as their guide.

These are just some of the questions parents need to discuss. Of course there are many more. The point, however, is that if you want to be an effective parent, you and your partner need to agree on exactly how you want to bring your children up and what set of values you intend using for that purpose. Again, the keyword is consistency.

"The keyword is consistency."

At this stage it is worth pausing to reflect on your own values, and ask your partner to do likewise. Are your values the same? How do they differ? Is there room for compromise? What other important matters need discussion — such as what time children should go to bed, use of the computer, access to the Internet and mobile phones?

THE BUILDING BLOCKS

Most parents would agree on what they want for their children: a happy, healthy, rewarding life; fulfilment of their potential; to be liked by other people; and to be a law-abiding citizen contributing to the society in which they live. Of these, happiness is possibly the single most valuable attribute and one which, if you believe the Dalai Lama, is open to us all — with training. As parents, our job is to provide this training, and to do this we need to teach children limits and boundaries, acceptable behaviour, respect and understanding of the need for rules, self-regulating behaviour and, above all, the principle of cause and effect — to accept the consequences of their actions.

There are numerous ways in which these can be achieved, and you should ideally start putting them into practice from birth. However, if you have come to this book at a time when your child is a little older, don't worry. It's not too late to start now, though the older the child the harder it may be to reorder some of your and their ideas!

These building blocks will be discussed at greater length in subsequent chapters, but here is a thumbnail sketch of some of the principal ones.

Teaching acceptable behaviour

Nobody likes a badly behaved child. Right from the start children need to learn what is considered acceptable behaviour and what is not.

- Read your children stories that teach them how to deal with feelings appropriately.
- Talk to them about what is acceptable and what is unacceptable, and listen to their ideas.
- Help children talk about what *they* are feeling and help them to find healthy ways of dealing with those feelings.
- Ask questions that help children to express how they think other people might feel if they were on the receiving end of unfair treatment.

Teaching respect and the need for rules

If there were no rules in a rugby match, the game would quickly descend into a free-for-all where someone might get hurt. So it is in everyday life. We need to know the rules of the society in which we live and how to respect other people.

- Discuss and explain rules ahead of time, not after the event (eg 'Click, clack front and back' and the need for seat belts in cars).
- Read stories that help with understanding of rules (eg road safety stories).
- Read stories that develop a sense of morality and justice.
- Play games that have rules and opportunities for taking turns.
- Discuss the rules of the road.
- Discuss keeping yourself safe and the rights of others.
- Discuss other rules you would like as a family — including rules for Mum and Dad.

Teaching self-awareness

It is equally important for children to know how they are feeling. In addition to contributing to acceptable behaviour, this self-knowledge will also help them to keep safe and improve self-esteem.

- Play tactile games to get in touch with senses and emotions so children know when they do not feel 'good' or 'safe'.
- Encourage brainstorming and problem-solving skills so children can solve problems and get out of unsafe or scary situations.

- Encourage children to talk about what is on their minds.
- Give lots of positive attention and genuine praise throughout the day, every day.

Never miss an opportunity to praise and encourage your children and, to borrow a key phrase from Triple P (Positive Parenting Program), developed in Australia by Professor Matthew Sanders and his colleagues from the Parenting and Family Support Centre at the University of Queensland: 'Catch your child being good!'

"Never miss an opportunity to praise and encourage your children."

Nurturing your child's spirit

To be a successful parent, we need to nurture our children's spirit, not constantly criticise and beat them down in the name of good behaviour, or as it is so often put, 'for their own good.' One of the most important ways in which we can build up (and equally, knock down) a child's spirit is with the language we use. For a child to know that they are loved and cared for no matter what, we need to use clear, positive, non-judgmental language. This is not always easy, especially when a child is being particularly annoying. However, a calm and consistent response to inappropriate behaviour will, in the end, be the most effective way of dealing with it.

"A calm and consistent response to inappropriate behaviour is the most effective way of dealing with it."

It is easy to break a child's spirit. Do that and you will create a massive rod for your own back. The following lists give some examples of how to break a spirit and how to build one up.

Breaking a child's spirit

- 'You're stupid.'
- 'You're a dummy.'
- 'You are so slow.'
- 'You're uncoordinated.'
- 'You're hopeless at maths.'
- 'You're always losing things.'
- 'You never listen.'
- 'You always forget your homework.'
- 'You're not very good at sport.'
- 'You don't have curly hair like your sister.'
- 'Why can't you be tidy like your brother.'

Building a child's spirit

- 'Well done, you're the best hugger!'
- 'I love your smile.'
- 'Good try.'
- 'Thanks for helping.'
- 'You're great with animals.'
- 'I liked the way you played with your cousin today.'
- 'You're such a good listener.'

- 'Thanks for waiting for me to finish on the phone.'
- 'Granny loved the card you made.'
- 'You have really nice friends.'
- 'You know a lot about trains.'

Seems simple really, doesn't it? But you'd be surprised how often, in the heat of family life, we forget to say these simple, life-affirming things and how ready we are to criticise and knock people down, even our own children.

There is another easy way to break a child's spirit: by being unfair. Children have an enormous sense of fairness and justice, and consequently are greatly hurt by actions they consider to be unfair or unjust. Children are like sponges, they soak up and react to their environment.

Another way in which a child's spirit can be broken is if they feel unloved or unwanted. In this busy, busy age when parents are hardworking and trying to make ends meet, it is often easy to forget that your children need a lot of your time if they are to learn the things they need to grow up as balanced and confident youngsters. It's understandable. You're tired, it's been a long day at the office, there's much to be done at home . . .

Here's a short parable which we offer without comment.

A man came home from work late again, tired and irritated, to find his five-year-old son waiting for him at the door.

'Daddy, may I ask you a question?'

'Yeah, sure, what is it?' replied the man.

'Daddy, how much money do you make an hour?'

'That's none of your business! Why do you ask?' the man said angrily.

'I just want to know. Please tell me, how much money do you make an hour?' pleaded the little boy.

'If you must know, I make twenty dollars an hour.'

'Oh,' the little boy replied, head bowed. Looking up, he said, 'Daddy, may I borrow ten dollars, please?'

The father was furious. 'If the only reason you wanted to know how much money I make is just so you can borrow some to buy some silly toy or some other nonsense, then you march yourself straight to your room and go to bed. Think about why you're being so selfish. I work long, hard hours every day and don't have time for such childish games.'

The little boy quietly went to his room and shut the door. The man sat down and became even more angry about the little boy's questioning. How dare he ask such questions only to get some money? After an hour or so, the man had calmed down and started to think he may have been a little hard on his son. Maybe there was something he really needed to buy with that ten dollars, and he really didn't ask for money very often. The man went to the door of the little boy's room and opened the door.

'Are you asleep, son?' he asked.

'No, Daddy, I'm awake,' replied the little boy.

'I've been thinking, maybe I was too hard on you earlier,' said the man. 'It's been a long, hard day and I took my aggravation out on you. Here's that ten dollars you asked for.'

The little boy sat straight up, beaming. 'Oh thank you, Daddy!' he cried. Then, reaching under his pillow, he pulled out some more crumpled-up notes.

The man, seeing that the boy already had money, started to get angry again. The little boy slowly counted out his money then looked up at the man.

'Why did you want more money if you already had some?' the father grumbled.

'Because I didn't have enough, but now I do,' the little boy replied. 'I have twenty dollars now. Can I buy an hour of your time?'[2]

It is vital to make time for our children.

2

shaping
your baby's
personality

H aving given much thought to the matter, you have decided to go ahead and have a baby. Imagine that you have been through the painful bit and there you are cuddling a brand-new little baby. All innocence, sweetness and light, the little face gazes up at you knowingly. What countless ages of wisdom are already stored in that tiny brain? What does the future hold for your precious infant?

Then you remember Tom, your other child. He's just entered the Terrible Twos and already he has the destructive power of an international rugby scrum. Only a week ago you had to rescue the cat from him. It had been a close call, with pussy very nearly disappearing down the drain. You need eyes in the back of your head every minute of the day with that one! It's all go, go, go. Hyperactivity *in extremis*. Will little Amy turn out to be like that? 'Oh, God, I hope not,' you sigh quietly.

And the strange thing is, she probably won't. Same parents, same environment, but a totally different personality. The key to this, it would appear, is the experience Amy had in the womb. Much research has been done in this area. In particular, following extensive research into the growth and development of children *in utero*, Dr Thomas

Verny, in his remarkable book *The Secret Life of the Unborn Child*, came to the conclusion that a foetus can see, hear, experience, taste and, on a primitive level, even learn. Most importantly, perhaps, the foetus can also feel. Consequently, all these sensations in the womb begin shaping the baby's personality.[3] Without going too deeply into it here, it is safe to say that there is now ample evidence that the feelings of the mother during pregnancy can have a vital effect on her unborn child. Chronic anxiety throughout pregnancy can, for example, result in the child developing an anxious personality after birth.

It's not only mothers who have an effect, fathers play their bit, too. How a father feels and reacts to his wife's pregnancy has a significant role in determining the success or otherwise of that pregnancy. For a long time, fathers were largely ignored in the pre-birth scenario, but, increasingly over the past couple of decades, research has shown that the emotional state of the father plays a vital part in the eventual personality of the child.

Now conversely, of course, a joyful, happy pregnancy full of laughter and a relaxed attitude will play an enormous part in producing a happy, relaxed, non-fussing baby.

This is important knowledge, because to some extent it allows parents to be pre-warned about their child's personality formation. Studies done with children who underwent severe stress in the womb have shown, for example, that they are more likely to suffer emotional and physical disorders than babies from stress-free pregnancies. Please don't be unnecessarily alarmed if you had a pretty stressful pregnancy, however, because your baby may well turn out to be perfectly fine, but it could be helpful to be on the look-out as the child grows for signs that may indicate some emotional or physical unrest — the sooner you identify it, the sooner you can address it.

So, little Amy has now been born and comes into the harsh glare of the world already programmed to some extent. She has made certain decisions about the world into which she has been born based on the sort of reactions Mum had to outside stimuli, and will hold these unconscious beliefs until taught otherwise. From day one this learning process will accelerate.

TONES OF VOICE

Tones of voice, indistinct but nevertheless discernable in the womb, are suddenly clearer. The raised voice that caused Mum's pulse to race and the oxygen supply to the placenta to be diminished, causing a certain amount of distress to Amy, now becomes louder and clearer. She relates it to the cutting off of her air supply and reacts violently by screaming. The soft tinkle of laughter or the cooing sigh of happy acceptance, on the other hand, is taken as a sign by Amy that she can relax and that all's well with her world.

TOUCH

Touch is another important factor in the development of Amy's personality at this time. Babies like to be touched and stroked. It's not until they reach their early teens that they'll start backing away from nice sloppy kisses from Mum and Dad and their siblings! Deprive a child of these tactile sensations at an early age and you are asking for trouble in the years to come. Incidentally, it is worth noting here that children born by caesarean section may grow up demanding a lot of physical contact as a result of the subconscious desire for the tactile experience they were denied by not having to fight their way through the birth canal. With more and more caesarean births these days, here is one behavioural trait you can observe and compensate for at an early age. It is important that mothers of babies born in this way get to hold and cuddle their child as soon as possible after birth.

SIGHT

Sight is the third important sensation that all babies need for the development of a healthy personality. Colourful mobiles over the bed, cheery paintings on the nursery walls — these are some of the building blocks of a cheery personality. Lacklustre rooms with little or no colour deprive a baby of important stimulation and can contribute to producing a dull personality.

Amy also needs something else from you at this time: she needs to see a reaction from you. Since your reaction to her is her only yardstick at this stage of her life, it is important that you do not ignore her when she attempts to engage with you. Make funny noises when she sticks her finger in your eye. Clap your hands when she smiles or waves her teddy in the air. This makes

Amy feel that she is achieving something, that she is controlling at least a tiny part of her life, and this becomes even more important as Amy develops into a toddler. By failing to react when she tries to do something, she will soon gain the impression that she cannot succeed and will give up. This is known as 'enforced helplessness' and may have an effect on the child later, and, in particular, the part of the brain that makes them empathic may not develop. In cases of profound emotional neglect, capacity to feel empathy may be irretrievably lost, and some doctors believe that in some cases substance abuse and adolescent violence can be linked to such early life experiences.

"There is no one 'correct' way to parent a child."

So what are the building blocks of personality that we have gathered together so far?

> Amy needs to hear ...
> *Soft, happy tones*

> Amy needs to feel ...
> *Gentle, soothing touches*

> Amy needs to see ...
> *Bright, cheerful colours*

Right from birth, our parenting styles are important. Let us say at the outset that there is no one 'correct' way to parent a child. Children aren't like video recorders — you can't just program them according to the manual. There are a million variations and, apart from the obvious, nobody has a right to tell you that the way you are bringing up your child is wrong. It is important, however, that you feel confident and that the way you choose to parent your child feels right to you, even if it is frowned upon by your mother-in-law!

HOW YOUR BEHAVIOUR CAN AFFECT YOUR BABY

Various actions on your part will trigger particular responses in your baby and it is worthwhile stopping for a moment to think about these.

Let's take Amy as an example, and the neighbour's newborn baby, Tristan. When Amy was first born, her mum decided to breastfeed her on demand. Amy would niggle, get a feed and a nappy change, and go back to sleep. Tristan's mum, on the other hand, decided to stick rigidly to a program of four-hourly feeds. This didn't always please Tristan, who would cry, and sometimes scream, if he got hungry. But still he had to wait for the allotted feeding time.

If this went on for too long it could have resulted in Tristan feeling that he had to scream and make a fuss every time he wanted his needs met, whereas little Amy may well have thought that the world was a pretty OK place and that all she had to do was wait patiently and all her needs would be met.

The question of when to feed your baby is a much-argued one, with mothers like Amy's lined up on one side of the fence, and lots of mums like Tristan's lined up on the other. One side will argue that feeding on demand only sets up bad habits in the child and results in over-tired mothers, while the other side says that it is cruel to allow babies to cry and that they shouldn't be allowed to go hungry.

When you feed your baby and the method you use to feed is entirely your own choice. Nevertheless, introducing some sort of routine and training your baby to stick to a more sociable timetable may be beneficial for both parents and baby.

To add to Tristan's problems, his cot was placed in a sterile room with no pictures on the walls and no books or toys on display. Neither of his parents talked to him much, let alone read him stories or played music to him.

Next door, Amy's cot was surrounded by interesting things to look at, a brightly coloured fish mobile hung over her head and there was always someone close at hand to play peekaboo with her.

As the two children grew up, the different parenting styles became more noticeable. Tristan rarely got a cuddle from his dad, who thought it unmanly to cuddle boys, and his mum gave little more than the cursory kiss. He was criticised for the smallest misdemeanour and there were even times when he had to go without a meal as a punishment. While next door, Amy was always being told how special she was and being praised for even the simplest task she completed. The family would chat away at mealtimes, which were at the same time practically every day, and if Amy ever said she felt sad or angry, her parents would listen and acknowledge her feelings. She was allowed to make mistakes without repercussions, so she was willing to take risks and experiment, and consequently learned faster. We could go on, but you can see the point.

MEETING YOUR BABY'S NEEDS

It is essential for a baby's needs to be met. Meeting these needs will influence the intrinsic nature of the child in later life. What are those needs?

- Being valued
- Being heard
- Being loved
- Being fed
- Being wanted
- Above all, feeling safe and secure

As we mentioned before, there is no one 'right' way to bring up a child, so long as everything we do, we do with love, clarity, consistency and without manipulation.

"Children soak up everything around them and store it for later repetition."

If you take the analogy of children being like sponges, they soak up everything around them and store it for later repetition. You know yourself that anything you learned between the ages of five and 15 you can probably remember far better today than something you only learned a month ago. The Jesuits knew what they were talking about when they said, 'Give me the child until he is seven and I will show you the man.'

BONDING

Vital to the wellbeing of a newborn baby is bonding, the cementing of the relationship, both physical and emotional, between mother and baby. During the bonding process, the baby feels protected, loved and wanted, and this will generally extend into later life. This equally applies to men. The male equivalent of bonding is called engrossment. It is important that fathers spend as much time as possible with their newborn children in order to form the same sort of bond between them that the baby shares with its mother.

In extreme cases where there is no bonding with either Mum or Dad, a condition known as marasmus may occur. If the baby receives no love and affection, no cuddles and no attention, then it may pine away and die. This, however, is extremely rare today. There are many mothers who have found it difficult to bond with their babies, but manage to have perfectly reasonable relationships with them as they grow older. Still, if after some time you feel that the bonding process isn't working, do seek help.

What all this means is that you stand a better chance of being an effective parent if you started on the right footing. Interference in the mother–baby birthing process may make bonding harder, and may consequently affect the relationship.

In later chapters we will look in greater depth at the effects of parental attitudes and beliefs on children, the importance of play and other ways in which you can develop your child's potential. Meanwhile, it is crucial to examine one vital organ in your baby's body, and that is the brain.

3

the brain — understanding the hardware

I t is extremely helpful to know how your child's brain develops and what you can do to enhance that development, because within the brain lies the child's basic character. The physical development of a child is commonly measured using external indicators such as arms and legs, overall weight, and whether the child has rosy cheeks or shiny hair. Not much time is spent wondering how the baby's brain is growing inside that pretty little skull. That's probably because most parents don't fully appreciate the brain's development process.

For the purposes of determining character, it is useful to have a basic understanding of how your child's brain works, so here's a quick guide to the salient features.

The brain is to us humans what the CPU (central processing unit) is to a computer. It takes information in from the environment around it, processes that information and does what is necessary with it. Sometimes it will give other parts of the body instructions to behave in a particular way, and at other times the extremities of the body will give the brain feedback to help it send out the appropriate signals. Think what happens when you accidentally put your hand on a hot stove-top. In a nanosecond the hand has relayed a message to the brain, saying, 'Get me out of here, it's burning me.' A further nanosecond and the brain has relayed the information: 'Pick your hand up quick-smart!' Hundreds of muscles and nerves are involved in this split-second exercise, which is just one example of how our brains work for us every day and every night. Even when we are asleep the brain is still sending complex messages to the body, determining when the body should fall asleep, when it should wake up, controlling the bladder during sleep, and so on.

For the brain to function properly it needs three things: oxygen, water and integration. We tend to take oxygen for granted, but it is important to check the quality of the atmosphere in your home because bad air can make for bad brains. Obviously contaminants such as cigarette smoke and the smoke from open coal fires should be avoided where possible; and, if you happen to live in or near a heavily industrialised area or near a main road, you may want to use an ioniser to purify the air in your home.

"For the brain to function properly it needs three things: oxygen, water and integration."

THE IMPORTANCE OF DEEP BREATHING

It is also important to teach children how to breathe properly. Most of us are sloppy breathers. We tend to breathe in a very shallow way, using only the top third of our lungs. Ideally, we need to learn to breathe like opera singers — that is, to take in oxygen right to the bottom of our lungs each time we breathe in. In this way, we properly aerate the body and the brain.

WATER

Water is equally important. Children need to remain hydrated at all times and the best liquid for that purpose is water. Pure water hydrates. Once we add anything to it, such as cordial, fruit juice or tea, for example, we are changing the nature of the drink to a food type which needs digesting and it will not help to hydrate the brain as effectively.

Seventy-five per cent of the human body is made up of water, which, as we all learned at school, is an excellent conductor of electricity. What's that got to do with the brain, you ask? Well, the actions of the brain and nervous system are dependent on the conduction of electrical currents between the brain's various cells and the body's sensory organs. This is facilitated by water. The more water in your system, the better the brain works. It's as simple as that. If the brain is deprived of water then dehydration occurs and brain function is depleted until eventually, in extreme cases, the brain dies.

Stress and brain dehydration

One of the most common ways in which the brain dehydrates is through stress. The more stress the body is under, the drier the brain becomes. That's why it is important to drink plenty of water before sitting an exam or a test of any sort. The water hydrates the brain, working towards relieving some of the stress the brain is experiencing, which radically improves its function.

> *"Remember, the only liquid that hydrates the brain is water. All other liquids are processed by the body as food."*

INTEGRATION OF THE BRAIN

As we mentioned, the brain needs three things to function properly: oxygen, water and integration. Human brains are divided into three parts, which are:

- The reptilian brain (or brain stem)
- The midbrain (or mammalian brain)
- The cerebrum

Integration means ensuring that all three parts are working in harmony with each other, although we often use only some of our brain — which accounts for the many different behaviours we encounter in people. Indeed there are times when we use only one or two parts, depending on the task at hand. We need to have access to all three parts simultaneously, however, to learn easily and behave appropriately.

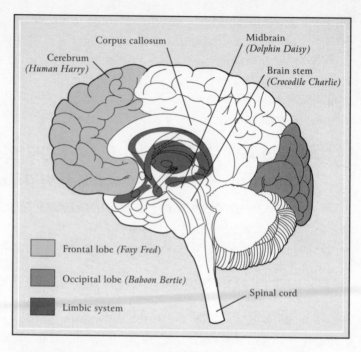

Corpus callosum

Midbrain
(Dolphin Daisy)

Cerebrum
(Human Harry)

Brain stem
(Crocodile Charlie)

Frontal lobe *(Foxy Fred)*

Occipital lobe *(Baboon Bertie)*

Limbic system

Spinal cord

IDENTIFYING THE THREE PARTS OF THE BRAIN IN YOUR CHILD

For easy identification, we have given each of these three areas special character names. We call the reptilian brain Crocodile Charlie and the mammalian brain Dolphin Daisy. The cerebrum, the thinking and reasoning part, we call Human Harry. Human Harry has two friends, because the cerebrum is divided into a left and right part; we call the left brain Lion Larry and the right brain Rhino Raymond. Each of these has their own peculiar characteristics, and if you watch your child closely you will be able to identify some or all of these characteristics and name them accordingly.

Brain stem: Crocodile Charlie

The brain stem, or reptilian brain, is found at the base of the brain and resembles the brain of a reptile. This is a common trait shared by all vertebrates, whether they slither on their tummies or walk upright on two feet. The first part of the brain to evolve, the sole function of the reptilian brain is survival. It receives sensory information from the environment and acts upon it in one of two ways. The choice is simple: either fight or flight. When we function only in the reptilian part of our brain, we are either aggressive — that's the fight part — or we are withdrawn — the flight option. Both these are instinctive and fairly primitive reactions.

There are times when our children function solely in this part of the brain. Those are the times when they are either hitting, biting, running away when sad, clinging excessively to you, sulking or refusing to talk about what is on their mind.

Equally there are times when adults function in this part of the brain — probably not often, but those rare times when you yell at your children, or verbally abuse them by being snappy and short-tempered. All this is perfectly natural human behaviour, but indicates that you are working out of only one portion of your sophisticated brain. Charlie doesn't know how to respond, he just simply reacts.

Midbrain: Dolphin Daisy

The mammalian brain, or midbrain, was the next part of the brain to develop in the evolutionary process. Sitting just above the brain stem, the midbrain accommodates about nine different functions. Mammals have this part of the brain, in addition to the reptilian portion, enabling them to feel and remember. In the animal world the most obvious examples are probably dolphins and whales, who are particularly sensitive to their environment and respond to its changes rather than simply reacting to them. You could never, for example, train a snake to take a message to a neighbouring property, but dolphins have been trained to carry messages over thousands of kilometres of sea.

Residing in the midbrain is the limbic system, which is vital to the development of your child. It is the seat of all emotions, motivation, conscience and the first link to memory. Research has revealed that learning and appropriate behaviour is driven by a connection to this system, as it attaches feelings to particular activities and lessons, then translates them in a meaningful way to be stored as memory. Emotions and feelings originating in the limbic system, such as anger, fright, passion, love, hate, joy and sadness, are all mammalian inventions.

The limbic system also commands certain behaviours for the wellbeing of all mammals. It allows us to distinguish between the agreeable and the disagreeable, and to develop specific functions such as the one that induces females to nurse and protect their young. According to research by the director of the Amen Clinic for Behavioural Medicine in Fairfield, California, Dr Daniel Amen, females, on average, have a larger limbic system than males. This gives females several advantages — and disadvantages. Due to the larger limbic brain, most women are better able to express their feelings than men. They have an increased ability to bond and be connected to others, which is why women are the primary caregivers for children — there is no society on earth where men are predominantly primary caregivers. Females have a more acute sense of smell, which is likely to have developed from an evolutionary need for the mother to recognise her young. Having a larger limbic system leaves females somewhat more susceptible to depression, especially at times of significant hormonal changes such as the onset of puberty, after the birth of a child and at menopause.[4]

Dolphin Daisy can be gentle, thoughtful and considerate of other people's feelings. She knows and understands pretty well what her own feelings are and can express them. She is highly motivated, takes responsibility for her actions and will accept the consequences when she does something wrong. She is honest, and can often be extremely emotional and sensitive. However, Daisy is the first link to memory, so if she is not engaged she will genuinely have no memory of previous activity. For example, a thief who doesn't have Daisy engaged in his mind will deny any wrongdoing because he genuinely cannot remember doing it! Likewise, children who 'forget' to pick up their toys often genuinely cannot remember being told, and students who 'forget' to do their homework may genuinely not remember.

Cerebrum: Human Harry

The third part of the triune brain is known as the cerebrum, the part of the brain that distinguishes human beings from all other forms of life. This is the part that allows us rational, logical, linguistic and altruistic thinking.

Human Harry is a combination of his mates Lion Larry and Rhino Raymond. Harry functions best when both Larry and Raymond are integrated (see pages 52–54 for more information), so they are able to find solutions that are appropriate and functional. Together they provide Harry with ease of learning and appropriate behaviour.

Thanks to his cerebrum, Human Harry can think abstractly or in fine definition. He can make generalisations or be specific. He is capable of decision-making and is receptive to the ideas of others. He can express himself logically and clearly, remember the lessons he learns as he goes through life and, above all, he can reason.

The cerebrum is divided into two hemispheres, the left and the right brain, and each of these parts has a unique set of attributes.

Lion 'Left-Brain' Larry

Here's a little guy who can be utterly logical, is quite at home with sequential numbering, and loves facts and details. In short, he's exactly the sort of fellow that you'd want around the house to do odd jobs or be by your side when there are specialised tasks to be done.

Larry is good at making lists, finishing what he starts, and is most probably the guy who tidies his room and keeps all his toys in good order. What Larry is not so good at is seeing the big picture. He would much rather break it down into its constituent parts and examine those one at a time.

Things are more logical that way. He can also be stubborn, critical and judgmental.

> ## *"We generally only use about 20 per cent of our brains at any one time."*

Rhino 'Right-Brain' Raymond

Right-Brain Raymond is the exact opposite of Larry. He is the dreamy, illogical one. He is good to have around in times of crisis because he can see the big picture, and while Lion Larry is breaking the crisis down into its constituent parts, Raymond is looking for the solution! However, he can often have difficulty focusing his attention on the matter in hand because he is looking at that big picture rather than bothering with the minute details. Raymond is the creative one and is likely to become an artist, a writer or an actor. He's the one who will come up with interesting solutions to problems — which is why you won't find too many Raymonds in the public service!

Well, that's the brain as we have it. Although 100 per cent of it is available to all of us at all times, the fact is that we generally only use about 20 per cent of our brains at any one time.

UNDERSTANDING WHY YOUR CHILD BEHAVES IN A CERTAIN WAY

We have spent this time explaining the anatomy of the brain because once you become aware of the different types of behaviour the brain causes, you will be better able to recognise which part of the brain your child is using at any particular time and can orchestrate your response accordingly. This is especially so when you have children with recurrent behaviours. It is easy to despair in such cases, but once you understand where they are coming from, you can actively help them to modify the behaviour.

In the next chapter we will explain how you can get your child to access all parts of their brain, and in particular how they can access both the right and left sides of their cerebrum.

4

the brain — understanding the software

As we discussed in the previous chapter, if you have some basic knowledge of how your child's mind works and where they are coming from, you can more effectively address their behaviour. In this chapter we look in more detail at the brain's function to help you understand the processes.

Human Harry (the cerebrum) has two sides to his brain, Lion Left-Brain Larry and Rhino Right-Brain Raymond, each of which creates wildly different thought patterns. You have probably heard of this as left-brain and right-brain thinking — people say that they are either left-brain or right-brain thinkers. This isn't possible; it's just that they choose to use one side of Harry more often than the other.

These two characters have a strong influence on our day-to-day thought patterns and will be the driving force behind whether your son is going to be a pro footballer or a concert pianist, or your daughter a painter or a corporate lawyer.

Sometimes we work out of only one side of the brain, sometimes out of both. For example, you might be thinking of taking up mountain climbing. Right-Brain Raymond is all for it. 'Go on,' he urges, 'you can do it!' Then Left-Brain Larry chimes in: 'Don't be silly. You know you're terrified of heights. Don't go there!' This internal conversation will carry on in your head until one side wins.

ACCESSING BOTH SIDES OF THE BRAIN

Accessing both sides of the brain allows for a balanced approach to any subject. But how do you do it? Well, the technical answer is by crossing the corpus callosum. The corpus callosum is a very thick bundle of nerve fibres which connect the left and right hemisphere of the cerebral cortex, or Human Harry as we know him. In the 18th century, the corpus callosum was thought to be the site of the soul, and early in the 20th century it was unglamorously downgraded to the mere role of preventing the cerebral hemispheres from collapsing onto each other. It was only in the 1950s that the corpus callosum was finally discovered to have the vital function of transferring information between the two hemispheres.

Let's go back to the mountain-climbing analogy for a minute. Right-Brain Raymond has come up with this seemingly ludicrous suggestion, while Left-Brain Larry immediately wants to check out all the facts and find a logical way of approaching the situation. Raymond will put all the facts into a big picture and find a creative solution to the approach, and as Larry and Raymond keep talking to one another, the project moves forward easily. But what happens if one side refuses to take part in the conversation, or decides to pack it in halfway through? Well, you can guess, can't you? If Larry is the one who chucks it in, the chances are that you are going to rush off and join a mountaineering expedition without giving it much further thought and it won't be until you're somewhere near Mount Everest that you suddenly realise you aren't very fond of heights!

On the other hand, if it's Raymond who quits, then you sit and mull over all the things that might happen to you — broken ropes, avalanches, sherpas having heart attacks on the summit, and a whole host of other ghastly mishaps. Soon you decide that mountaineering is for the birds and give it away in preference for a nice game of bridge.

The importance of left and right brains

Why is it so important to use both sides of our brains? Well, for one thing, we wouldn't be able to read if we didn't. The left brain sees the words in order and the right brain searches the memory bank looking for the meaning of those words. Without using both sides of the brain your child would not be able to do any mathematics. Here the left brain determines the sequence and the right brain finds the solution. Nor would they be able to aspire to great artistic endeavour as it is the left brain that knows how to draw and the right brain that fills in the colour and provides all the flashy and creative bits.

If we are only able to access one side of our brain we quickly become unbalanced. If we use only the left brain, we become picky, fussy, over-cautious, obsessive, critical of other people and ideas, fanatical and stressed. If only the right brain is accessed, then we become dreamy, unable to concentrate, have no concept of time, take silly risks and tend to doodle a lot. Like butterflies, we flutter from one project to another.

This is where it is extremely helpful to understand the working of your child's brain. You can determine which side of the brain they are working out of at any given time and take steps to balance their thinking. If your son suddenly becomes very fussy about the food you put in front of him, or develops a great negative streak, for example, you can tell that he is working predominantly out of his left brain — and you can take action to help him work out of both sides. If the teachers report that your daughter has become very dreamy in class, and is always late, then the chances are she is working mostly out of her right brain. How do you tell when they are working out of both sides of their brain? They will be relaxed, get their work done in time and without undue stress; sometimes they will be logical and follow instructions well, and sometimes do things creatively, bringing in ideas of their own.

We all have the capacity to use both sides, or just one at a time, and of course there are times when we can benefit from using only the one side. For example, when we have a lot of instructions to follow, it helps to work out of the left brain, as it does when we are asked to give a considered opinion about something or when we wish to decide on whether a course of action is too risky. In short, when we are called upon to use our judgment. If, on the other hand, we wish to be creative — design some new clothes or lay out a garden — then we need the right brain. The right brain will also help us to be receptive to new ideas and respond to other people openly and without criticism. When children are well integrated and balanced, both sides of their brain will work together to decide which one needs to be dominant and which will take a back seat. Neither side disappears completely, however.

"We all have the capacity to use both sides of our brains."

BRAIN GYM: EXERCISING YOUR CHILD'S BRAIN

You probably already know this, but the brain is a muscle. As such it needs exercising, just like all the other muscles in your body. When we want to improve our biceps or our triceps, we go to the gym and exercise them daily. The same can be true of the brain, except that, instead of going to your local fitness centre, you can use 'brain gym' movements. Sounds odd, we know, but it works in exactly the same way.

Brain Gym is a series of specific movements designed to stimulate different parts of the brain so that they can do their job properly. The movements clear the neurological pathways of any blockages, releasing trapped stress so that the person can function at their best. These movements are the invention of the Educational Kinesiology Foundation, founded by Dr Paul Dennison, a teacher, and his wife, Gail, a dancer, in California nearly 20 years ago.[5] Many teachers in various parts of the world, including Australia and New Zealand, are now increasingly using these techniques in their classrooms, and within the next five years they will be commonplace in most of our schools on a daily basis to help pupils learn more easily.

How children learn to use the whole brain

Infants are in a natural state of learning. They are totally responsive to their immediate and caregiving surroundings, taking in tremendous amounts of information and transforming it into speech and action in a remarkably short period of time. If the infant is free to move, explore, see and make sounds, learning occurs to the extent that the child receives the love and feedback that reward its efforts.

Movement is the child's first teacher — they move instinctively in response to the unspoken question: *Where am I in space?* This is the first of four developmental areas of awareness.

The answer to *where* is achieved through coordination of muscular feeling and brain receptors in the inner ear. The child's eyes and hands open to the surrounding world.

Then there is the question: *Where am I in relation to objects in my environment?* Only through movement can the body store the spatial mapping information that will answer this question.

What is it? the child then asks. To know this, the *what* must build on *where*. The visual, auditory and tactile senses need to work together with the kinesthetic intelligence. As these questions are answered through the experience of movement, the child can free their intelligence to explore *Who am I?*

How Brain Gym supports 'whole brain' learning

There are four categories of Brain Gym movements, each addressing a different function of the brain and a different one of the four developmental areas of awareness mentioned in italics above. Brain Gym can help the learner to reactivate the 76 visual, auditory and motor patterns existing from birth that make learning easy and natural.

Brain Gym is a 'readiness' program: it prepares students of all ages to practise and master the skills for the mechanics of learning. The program includes a simple teaching format, a language for stress-free learning and a series of movements for integrating learning into the physiology, and is distinctive in that it addresses the physical, rather than mental, components of learning.

Using specific Brain Gym strategies, reading, writing, spelling, mathematics, communication and organisational skills can be improved. For many children this can also result in increased self-esteem, increased motivation and improved behaviour.

Many people were somewhat sceptical about Brain Gym when it first appeared, but numerous studies have proved that it works. One such study was carried out between 1989 and 1990 by Carla Hannaford, an educator and neurophysiologist, on Hawaiian fifth-grade students. Hannaford implemented a year-long program incorporating Brain Gym in the classroom. Pre and post tests were completed using the Brigance Inventory of Basic Skills[6] and results showed a one- to two-year growth for more than 50 per cent of the students on mathematics scores — which was greater than had been expected. Behaviour patterns also greatly improved.

Closer to home, Peter Whetton, senior Special Education instructor at Christies Beach High School in South Australia, implemented this project over three terms, publishing his *Longitudinal Perspective on Brain Gym: Outcomes with Special Ed Students, Australia* in 1987. The purpose of the project was to determine whether the inclusion of Brain Gym movements would have an effect on the behaviour, coordination, attention span or academic skills of high school students in a Special Education classroom.

In part one of the study, 12 students were divided into four groups: the Brain Gym group or one of three control groups. The results showed that the Brain Gym group improved markedly in all areas; the two control groups using movement showed small areas of improvement; and the control group with no movement showed no improvement.

In part two of the study, all students chose to do only Brain Gym for a nine-week period. Results showed continued improvements. In part three, Brain Gym was not used in the classroom for an eight-week period. Results showed that skills and behaviours declined until Brain Gym was reintroduced. A comparison with the participants' abilities over the previous four years showed an average age growth of four to five years in reading, maths and spelling, and more than seven years' growth in comprehension.

The results of various experiments with the students showed:

- Improvement in writing and spacing of work
- Increased focus during group times
- Increased self-awareness
- Increased confidence in spelling, maths and writing
- Improvement in reading
- Improved organisation and productivity in set-work assignments
- Generally the students were calmer, happier and less moody

In everyday terms this means that doing Brain Gym movements regularly with your young children at home will result in at least some of the above, in addition to which behaviour will be more manageable and learning will become more effortless.

Some useful Brain Gym movements

To gain the maximum benefit from Brain Gym, aim to practise it with your children on a daily basis for five minutes every morning if you can spare the time. As we have said, it is a preventative process rather than a remedial one, one that will have a beneficial and lasting effect on both your child's learning ability and behaviour. Children who exhibit inappropriate behaviours such as biting, kicking or general aggressiveness can benefit from Brain Gym movements, and certain movements can be used to calm an agitated child. They can be done anywhere, anytime.

The following are some of the more common movements and what they can achieve for your child:

Using both sides of the brain together (brain integration)

Cross Crawl involves your child marching around the room with the left elbow touching the right knee, alternating with the right elbow touching the left knee. Ask them to do this for about 3 minutes.

The Elephant also helps children overcome aggressive behaviour. Ask your child to stand and extend one arm, and then to press down their ear on to their extended arm as if it were glued to it. Pretending their arm is an elephant's trunk, ask them to look at their fingertips and with their 'trunk' draw a figure-eight lying on its side in the air — left to right, then back again. After a while the child can also practise writing simple words in the air with their 'trunk'. As the trunk moves, so should the whole body from the waist up and the child should be looking ahead past their fingertips, while following the movement of the trunk. This exercise should be done for a few minutes on each side.

For children who feel stuck or can't express themselves

Footflex helps to 'switch on' the language brain. It is particularly helpful when a child cannot find the right words, even though they may know the answer to a question. Ask the child to grasp the tender spots in the ankle, calf and behind the knee one at a time, while slowly pointing and flexing the foot. This should be done on each leg for about one minute.

Switching On is an effective energy exercise which will enhance quick thinking. Ask your child to do the following: While holding the navel with one hand, rub just below the collarbone to the right and left of the breast bone with the other hand for about 10 seconds. Then, keeping the hand on the navel, hold two fingers under the lower lip and breathe, then move the two fingers above the upper lip. This should be done for about 10 seconds. Next, move the fingers from the upper lip to the tail bone, again for about 10 seconds.

To help children who are overactive, confused or angry

Hook-Ups can help calm a child in no time. Done in two parts, this movement is particularly helpful with hyperactive children. First, ask the child to sit on a chair with their legs extended, then place their left ankle over the right one. Then they should interlace their fingers by crossing their hands right over left and then draw the hands in and up to the chest. Ask them to sit like this for one minute, breathing deeply, with their eyes down and tongue on the roof of the mouth.

For the second part, uncross the legs and put the fingertips of the two hands together, continuing to breathe deeply for another minute.

These are just some of the movements Brain Gym teaches and though they sound weird, there is a huge amount of research to prove that they really work. For more information you can visit www.braingym.org.

FOCUSING

Like being a spectator at a sports match, it's much more fun if you have some inkling of the rules and what the players rushing about the field are meant to be doing. So it is with children. If we have a broad idea of how their brains work and where they are coming from, in the long run they will be easier to deal with and more fun to have around.

There is just one more brain interaction we need to look at. This final aspect of the brain's function is the focus dimension. This involves crossing the line between the back, or occipital, brain and the frontal lobes. It is here that the all-important action of focus is carried out. Children who are under-focused tend to be inattentive, have difficulty in understanding concepts, may have some delay in language and appear to be hyperactive, flitting from one activity to the next, seemingly unable to concentrate. A child who is over-focused tends to try too hard and may become obsessive and compulsive, not listening and only seeing one thing at a time.

Once again, both front and back brains are equally important when in balance. To add to our menagerie, we will call these two Foxy 'Front-Brain' Fred and Baboon 'Back-Brain' Bertie.

So what are the attributes of these two?

Foxy Fred is over-focused and pays great attention to detail. He therefore tends to be inflexible and cannot see anything other than what he is doing. He is unable to move on to the next activity because he has difficulty in seeing anything other than the task immediately to hand. He is often in trouble because he doesn't listen (in truth because he doesn't hear!). All this is fine if he's studying or doing detailed work, but not a great deal of help at other times.

Baboon Bertie is highly active, as his name suggests. He swings from one activity to another with the ease of a monkey swinging through the jungle. His visual perspective is wide and therefore he is easily distracted when something catches the corner of his eye.

He is constantly moving towards stimuli and it is these children who are often diagnosed as having ADD or ADHD (attention deficit hyperactivity disorder). Always on the go and fascinated by his environment, Bertie will have difficulty in focusing on any detail for more than a few seconds at a time.

As with the left and right brains, so too the front and back brains can work together in harmony or separately and against each other. Looking at your child, how do you know which part of the brain, front or back, they are working out of? Here's a quick guide to help you decide.

If the child is in Foxy Fred mode, watch out for:

- Great attention to detail
- Not being able to stop what they're doing
- Nagging about the same thing incessantly
- Not coming when called because they are playing
- Learning difficulties
- Not remembering something they were told a few minutes before
- Irrational arguments

If the child is in Baboon Bertie mode, watch out for:

- The child being easily distracted
- Not being able to focus
- Lacking all attention to detail
- Attraction to any stimuli within their peripheral vision
- Not being able to sit still

Children who exhibit these behaviours are working out of the back of their brains only and lack the integration which makes for a balanced mind and balanced behaviour.

BALANCING THE BRAIN

So how is this balance achieved? As before, one of the answers is Brain Gym. The two main concepts in this case are language and movement. To break Foxy Fred's over-focused state of mind, ask him a question about what he is doing. In order to answer you, he will have to search back and right brain for an answer and his focus is automatically broken. Only then can you introduce another idea to him. Movement is another good way to get Foxy Fred to pay attention. Get his eyes to move from side to side, preferably using something brightly coloured, like a picture in which he is interested. This way his concentration in what he was doing is broken and you can then suggest something different as his perspective is widened.

To break Baboon Bertie's loss of focused state, get him to look at something specific, or give him a specific task to do, usually a linear task, to engage his front brain and left brain and take him out of his broad perspective. For example, you might ask him to write the shopping list. Once he loses his wide perspective, Hook-Ups — the Brain Gym movement above — are useful to settle and calm him so he can stay in a balanced, focused mode.

5

the essence of
your child

N ow that you have some idea of how your child's brain functions, let's look again at the essence of your baby — this wonderful little sponge soaking up everything that is going on.

This sponge-like nature is what makes parenting such a challenge. If babies had a little switch in their backs like battery-operated dolls and could be turned off so that not everything we do affects them, then we could behave in any way we choose, say anything we wanted and treat them in any way we liked. This is obviously not the case. Their tiny antennae are constantly scanning for clues as to who they are, how they are valued and what their place is in the world. All these things affect how they feel and how they behave, and form the beliefs that will stay with them into later life, perhaps forever.

"Babies' tiny antennae are constantly scanning for clues as to who they are, how they are valued and what their place is in the world."

So these antennae are the origin of their core beliefs and values, the essence of the child.

Myra was determined to breastfeed her newborn son, Tom, as she had her other son for 14 months. After a few days it became obvious that Tom, who was tiny at birth, was clearly not interested and kept refusing the proffered breast. Myra kept persevering, Tom kept refusing, until finally a friendly nurse pointed out that he was starving and brought him a bottle. He latched on to it with great determination, then looked up into Myra's eyes — the start of a mutual understanding of his determination, which shows itself even now that he is in his twenties. He still will not take 'no' for an answer and if he wants something he will find a way of getting it. This attitude can be very challenging for a young mother, but once Myra acknowledged the trait she was able to manage it more constructively and he has grown into a positive young man.

So what is it about Tom that made him so different at that early stage from his older brother? It is his 'essence', his very fabric, the inside bits that are woven together to form a unique person. In a nutshell, it is the sum total of the sights and sounds that he picked up in his life and formed conclusions from in his own mind. It is a result of the messages he has received, from as early as his time in the womb.

MESSAGES IN THE WOMB

Dr Peter Fedor-Freybergh, when he was professor of Obstetrics and Gynaecology at Sweden's University of Uppsala, was one of the first experts to research and understand a baby's expectations in the womb. He discovered that a baby whose time in the womb was safe and pleasant expected the same of the outside world (despite the nasty shock many babies got from being forced through a narrow birth canal, then held up by their feet and smacked soundly on the bottom!). On the other hand, babies who had a rough time in the womb — subjected to loud noises and wild adrenalin rushes from mother — were less comfortable in the outside world.[7]

The first three years of a child's life are probably the most formative of all for it is during this time that the subconscious programming is taking place. If, for example, as a baby you received attention whenever you wanted it, if someone came whenever you cried, or picked you up and hugged you when you lay there gurgling happily, then you most likely formed the opinion that the world was a pretty safe and happy place in which to be. Sometimes you might have had to wait a bit and cry a bit longer before your needs were met, but if, when they were, you got a cuddle and a smile, then you most probably learned that there are times when you just have to withhold gratification, but nevertheless you were loved and wanted.

"The first three years of a child's life are probably the most formative of all."

On the other hand, if nobody paid any attention to you when you lay quietly in your cot, and you had to scream and bawl to get any attention, you might have come to the conclusion that you had to make a big fuss before you received any love and attention. Once attention was forthcoming, but given with irritation and annoyance, you might have considered it preferable to bottle up your feelings rather than risk Mum or Dad's disapproval. This is a basic survival instinct. A baby knows full well that they are entirely dependent on others for everything, and instinct dictates that it would be wise to do nothing to jeopardise that.

Babies cry because they need something. Either they want their nappy changed, or they are hungry or frightened, or, sometimes, they just want to be picked up and cuddled. They have no other way of communicating their wishes. There is absolutely nothing wrong in picking a child up when they cry. It demonstrates love and affection and tells the child that the world is basically a safe place in which to be. It ultimately helps the child to build good self-esteem and this will become vital as they grow up and become victim to a host of outside pressures.

"At this stage in a baby's life absolutely nothing you do can be considered as spoiling."

TWO KINDS OF MESSAGE

As children grow up they basically receive two different kinds of message from the world. One message will reflect their own needs and wishes, the other will conflict with them. They will either get the message that they can be themselves, follow their own inclinations, have their own interests, and eventually follow their own chosen careers. Allowed to follow this path, they will probably feel that it is OK to be themselves and that there is no need to go through life wearing a mask and pretending to be people they are not.

The other message tells children that basically they mustn't be themselves, but have to be different. This can be, for example, the case where the child is expected to conform to certain social and behavioural patterns within the family context and fulfil certain aspirations that are alien to their own beliefs and desires. All this can cause tremendous conflicts in their mind and affect the way they see themselves and the rest of world in which they are growing up. The Victorians were experts at filling their children with complexes. One of their favourite expressions was 'Children should be seen but not heard.' In essence, what they were saying was: 'If you must be here, the least you can do is pretend that you aren't!' In these more modern times, parents sometimes say to their children, 'Just do as you're told!' In other words, 'You have no place thinking for yourself, just do what we tell you and our lives will be much simpler.'

THE DANGERS OF CRITICISM

Criticism plays a very big part in this latter scenario and can have a disastrous effect on a child's self-esteem if delivered in the wrong way. Children of any age who are criticised generally behave in one of two ways. They either take the criticism to heart, feel inadequate and powerless and collapse in on themselves, their self-esteem badly damaged, or they become aggressive, fight back and are branded as rebellious, when probably all they are doing is asserting their right to be themselves. Very often we don't realise that we are criticising our children. We think we are trying to be constructive, but in reality they hear it as criticism. Here's a typical example: 'Sally, you are so untidy. Pick up your toys and put them in the cupboard, please.' Now Sally's mum wasn't meaning to be unkind to her daughter, but she was fed up with all her toys spread around the living-room floor. Sally, in all probability, hears the first sentence — 'You are so untidy' — and takes it to heart. She may or may not thereafter accede to her mother's request to pick up her toys. After all, she's untidy, isn't she? A better way of handling this would simply be to say, 'Sally, please pick up your toys and I'll help you put them away.'

"Try to avoid nagging!"

Nagging is another form of criticism we should also try to avoid. After a while children tend to ignore nagging, which ultimately means that they are likely to ignore the important things you are trying to tell them.

DANGEROUS UNCONSCIOUS MESSAGES

There are all sorts of messages hidden in the things we say to our children, most of which we don't really mean or are not even consciously aware of, but which children are quick to pick up on and construe in their own immature way. There are the 'don't exist' messages, 'grow up' messages and the 'stop being a nuisance' messages.

The effects of these messages on the essence of a child can result in the child feeling that they aren't good enough, then they feel inferior and low self-esteem creeps in. If left unchecked, this can have a disastrous effect on the rest of their lives. Low self-esteem is very often the root cause of relationship breakdowns, addictive behaviour, criminal intentions and a variety of other unfortunate circumstances.

The 'don't exist' message

What is a 'don't exist' message? Comments such as 'I could have been a doctor/lawyer/manager by now if you hadn't been born.' Janet had a heavy one laid on her at an early age. Her mother told her that she had always enjoyed good health up until the time that Janet was born, and had suffered poor health ever since. Not surprisingly, for a long time she blamed herself for her mother's ill-health, children being the susceptible little things they are, and if this belief had been strong enough and reinforced enough, there was a strong possibility she might have repeated the same pattern when she had a difficult time with her own child at birth.

The 'grow up' message

A common 'grow up' message — and how often have we all said it unthinkingly? — is 'Oh, stop being such a baby!' 'Just grow up, will you!' is another common one. The child simply construes this to mean 'Stop being yourself and be someone different.' Then, of course, there's that ghastly old adage 'Big boys don't cry!' translated as 'Stop feeling.'

The 'stop being a nuisance' message

'Stop being a nuisance' is a great way to dampen any child's enthusiasm. It may be a pain in the neck having to clear away all the pots and pans that they have pulled out from the kitchen drawer, but it is part of the important experimentation process of growing up. What you are saying in reality is: 'You are being selfish making more work for me. Stop experimenting and go away.'

MINOR CRITICISM

Then there are the day-to-day minor criticisms in which most of us indulge. For example, when a child chooses a particular dress or a pair of shoes they want to wear, we tell them to go and change. Why do we do it? What sort of message are they taking from this? Well, for a start, we are telling them they have bad taste and are wrong, though in truth we probably want them to change because we fear what other people might say if they see our children going out dressed in that manner. Maybe it doesn't quite conform with others. Who really makes the rules? Is it right to care that much, or are we only disempowering our children by behaving like this? After all, we can't really expect our children to learn to make decisions and be responsible when we are constantly withdrawing their power to do so.

On another occasion, the child may come back from school saying, 'I'm not as clever as the other kids.' 'Of course you are, darling,' we say in a well-meaning way. But what are we really telling them? That they are wrong and what they feel is invalid? We have no right to invalidate anybody's feelings. A better way to approach this scenario would be to say to your child: 'What happened at school today to make you feel that way? You sound like you are feeling a bit down this afternoon.' This gives the child the opportunity to talk about their feelings without in any way invalidating them.

This may all sound very far-fetched, but you'd be amazed by the way the average child's mind works. Anything that saps their self-esteem, however small, will set them back far more than we realise. Children grow up best when they are allowed to develop their own ideas and tastes. These don't necessarily have to be the same as ours, but, with love and guidance, our children will generally learn from our actions more so than our words. If we dress in a tasteful and colour-coordinated manner, the chances are so will they (well, until they become teenagers at least!). Most small children copy their parents and want to be like them, but first they have to feel good about themselves. Copying someone out of fear is the road to ultimate disaster, as it negates all value of self and can lead to problems in later life. Teenagers can be particularly susceptible to this and may be bullied into following someone down a destructive path that they might not otherwise have taken.

THE THREE As

There is a very simple method of combatting damaged self-esteem which we call the three As: Attending, Affection and Appreciation.

Attending

Attending means really listening to what your child is saying, and one of the best ways to demonstrate this is by making eye contact — which may mean squatting down to their eye level if they are very young. You know yourself that when you are speaking to someone, if they aren't looking at you then you feel they are not properly listening to what you are saying. Respond to your child's comments with 'who', 'what', 'where', 'when' and 'how' questions. These prolong the conversation and demonstrate that you are paying attention to what the child is telling you.

For example, a child runs excitedly into the room and says to Granny, 'I went to a birthday party today!' 'Oh, wow!' replies Granny.

This does not suggest that Granny is paying a great deal of attention. Instead, Granny could respond by saying something like 'Whose party was it?', 'What did you wear?', 'Did you play some fun games?', 'Who else was there?', 'What was the best part of the party?' This is the best way to have a conversation with a child and at the same time show the child that you are paying attention to what they are telling you.

Physically attending to your child is also important. It is preferable not to lean over a child when you talk with them, but rather sit down next to them. It indicates that you have time for the child, rather than just taking a passing interest. This may mean getting up and sitting down a hundred times a day — just look upon it as a form of exercise! The child is gaining immeasurably by it.

Affection

This means exactly what it says. All human beings need affection, and children particularly thrive on it and respond brilliantly. Lots of hugs, cuddles, stroking, massage, touching, holding, smiling — these are the ingredients for building good self-esteem and releasing the feel-good endorphins that nurture a child's spirit. Mix these with jokes and silly stories and try to create laughter whenever possible. All these things will help build happy and healthy children.

Appreciation

It is important to let a child know that they are valued. Every day they need to be reassured of their uniqueness, their value and their importance. Simple expressions like 'You have the best smile in the whole world', 'Gosh, you concentrate hard when you do that puzzle' or 'Thank you for helping me with the washing-up, I really appreciate it' are all that's needed to make a child feel special, important, valued and loved.

Be sincere, though — never say anything you don't mean.

6

the impact of
your own
attitudes and
beliefs

Parental attitudes and beliefs have an enormous effect on children. Without necessarily realising it, we imbue our youngsters with much of the conditioning we picked up from our parents — and so it goes back, generation to generation. When we have our first child, how many of us have said: 'I'm never going to do such-and-such like my mother did', or 'I'm not going to make my child eat so-and-so like I was made to', or made similar promises? And did it work? Go on, be honest!

In his magical book *The Prophet*, the Lebanese poet Kahlil Gibran wrote:

> *Your children are not your children.*
> *They are the sons and daughters of Life's longing for itself.*
> *They come through you but not from you,*
> *And though they are with you yet they belong not to you.*
> *You may give them your love but not your thoughts,*
> *For they have their own thoughts.*
> *You may house their bodies but not their souls,*
> *For their souls dwell in the house of tomorrow, which you*
> *   cannot visit, not even in your dreams.*

You may strive to be like them, but seek not to make them
like you.
For life goes not backward nor tarries with yesterday.
You are the bows from which your children as living arrows
are sent forth.
The archer sees the mark upon the path of the infinite, and
He bends you with His might that His arrows may go
swift and far.
Let your bending in the archer's hand be for gladness;
For even as he loves the arrow that flies, so He loves also the
bow that is stable.[8]

Now add to this the sentiments of the poet Philip Larkin, whom we quoted in Chapter 1, and you may get the picture that inflicting your ideas and your beliefs on your children is not necessarily a great thing to do. Nevertheless, as a parent, you are going to have an enormous effect on your child's life, so it is a good idea to get your own beliefs and attitudes straight, because inevitably many of them are going to rub off on your child.

One young mother put it this way: 'The other day I found myself telling my daughter she couldn't wear a particular dress to school — it was a party dress and it would be a pity if it were to get dirty. The minute I said it I realised it was my mother talking. Although, as a young woman, I vowed never to argue with my daughter on what she wears, I found myself repeating the same words my mother had used and her mother before her. The words I expressed were first created when new clothes were a heavy burden on the family finances, and washing was done by hand. The same does not apply today — there is always the washing machine handy and somebody else does the ironing for me. So I don't really care if she wears her party dress to school, but still I found myself expressing the same sentiments.'

COMING OFF AUTOMATIC PILOT

Choice is one of the central themes of this book. We tend to live on automatic pilot, repeating parental patterns *unless* we become conscious. This book strives to take you off automatic and make you realise that you have choices.

At this point it may be useful to remind you, the parents, that your first priority is to look after yourselves. If you don't, you will be no use to your partner or your children. So many young parents give up everything for their children. This is not noble at all; it is damaging to both themselves and the role model they are presenting. *Balance* is the key word here. Parents need to ensure that they remain healthy, eat well and exercise regularly. So often mothers say, 'I don't have time for exercise.' But when you look at their houses, they are immaculately clean. Clearly hours have gone into house-caring, when body-caring is really much more important. Health and exercise should come before even cleanliness, as fitness is related to mental health. When we are fit, healthy chemicals are produced that reduce depression and low self-esteem. Parents also need to create time to do something that gives them joy, that makes them feel alive and more than just a parent. Some people can get this going to work, but for those that don't, a hobby or sport is essential for wellbeing.

Secondly, and just as importantly, you have to make time for your partner to ensure that you maintain a healthy relationship. Make the time to go out alone with your partner on a fairly regular basis. It might just be an hour sitting over a drink on the balcony of your local pub once a week, but that time together, when you can catch up with each other uninterrupted by the clamour of tiny voices, is both magic and nurturing.

It is a common belief among parents (brought about largely by the ideas that we learned from our own parents) that, when you have children, your life as you knew it must stop and you must give your all for the wellbeing of your youngsters. This isn't the case at all.

Childhood patterning is such a strong influence that much of what we are doing and thinking today we learned through our parents as we grew up, even if we realise somewhere in our hearts that they are not all appropriate!

For example, it may sometimes feel as if we're carrying an inexplicable heavy weight that prevents us from being creative or from stepping out of the box in which we've been living. We might harbour great plans and extraordinary ideas, but somehow we keep plodding along in life and just never get around to fulfilling any of them. Why? Well, little voices in our head may be saying, 'You'll never make it. It's too difficult' or 'You might fail and then you'll know for certain that you're the failure you always thought you might be.' All these negative messages may be echoes of parental conditioning, messages your parents carried within themselves and passed down to you. These are all Larry Lion behaviours — the left brain constantly censoring any new opportunities to behave differently. Survival is also an issue here. Crocodile Charlie will fiercely defend any old beliefs and is afraid that new ideas may threaten his survival. Wherever they come from, these messages are straitjackets that prevent us from fully being ourselves. Many of us allow these (left-brain) voices to dominate and rule our lives, and, in turn, pass them down to our children, thereby robbing them of new ways of being.

POSITIVE AND NEGATIVE CONDITIONING

The following two cases demonstrate the limiting effects of negative conditioning, and just how positive conditioning can enhance our lives.

Case 1: Simon is a teenager. From an early age he has believed that people have been out to get him — his parents, his teachers, even his so-called friends. For many years, he has listened to his father coming home from work and complaining about how the boss has done the dirty on him, not given him the pay rise he was promised, given a plum job to another worker, and what a general, all-round untrustworthy piece of work he is. Coupled with this, Simon gets a good dose of detention from his teacher for fooling around in class, despite the fact that Simon always swears that it was the kid sitting next to him who started it and he was just an innocent bystander. His limbic system, or mammalian brain, is not engaged and therefore his centering dimension is not integrated.

'People are simply not to be trusted,' Simon has decided. 'The whole world is out to get me.' As a result, Simon has become fearful and suspicious, and, as he grows older, more neurotic.

Case 2: Jenny is a smiling, open-faced young girl with a kind word for everybody. Her father is a successful bookshop owner and her mother is a district nurse. Often, after school, Jenny helps her dad out in the shop and many of the book buyers stop to talk with her. When her mum comes home, she tells Jenny stories about the patients she has visited that day and how she has helped them to get better. 'People are kind and safe,' Jenny has decided. 'People are my friends.' The result of this is that Jenny is a relaxed, open and trusting young girl.

"Everything we do, see and say is a product of our conditioning."

The *Macquarie Dictionary* defines conditioning as 'a process by which a response is learned by coming to be associated with a particular stimulus, object or situation'. In essence, conditioning is a collection of our early messages, first from our parents, then teachers, then society at large. Everything we do, see and say is a product of our conditioning, and it is this conditioning that provides us with filters. Filters are really somebody else's reality — donated to us by our parents as a goodwill gesture. We often therefore have to fight for our own reality, since our conditioning involves seeing reality through our filters.

Filters to reality

What are these filters? Let's look at a couple of simple examples of early filters.

Lara is fed only four-hourly. Sally is fed on demand.

Lara's filter: She has to fight to have her needs met.
Sally's filter: Life is calm and her needs are attended to.

In Sam the toddler's home all ornaments are put away. In Toby the toddler's home all ornaments are left out.

Sam's filter: He learns there are things he may not touch.
Toby's filter: Toby is allowed to touch anything he sees.

Sometimes these messages are not very clear. Lara's mother means to stick to the four-hour feeding rule, but sometimes the screaming gets too much for her and she relents. Sam's parents may indeed put all the valuables out of reach or out of sight, but when Sam visits his grandparents, they allow him to touch their ornaments. So it is little wonder that by the time we are teenagers life as a whole proves to be confusing.

Stop here for a moment and think of some of the ways in which you think you were conditioned as a child. You might like to write them down for later reference. To help you start, here are some common conditioners:

- Rich people are greedy.
- Money is evil.
- Eat all your food, there are children starving in Africa.
- God will punish you if you think bad thoughts.

What were your parent's beliefs on the subjects of money, health, food, discipline and religion? Did they think it was tacky to talk about money? Did they talk about money all the time and relate everything to money? Did they think that you'd catch cold sitting in a draft? Did they think they wouldn't go to heaven if they missed going to church on Sundays?

Now, how do you think their attitudes and beliefs have affected you, and do you believe they are still warranted?

And, lastly, have you consciously passed any of these down to your children or given them the tools with which to make up their own minds on these matters?

The truth is that often we are operating on automatic pilot and are simply not aware of how these beliefs with which we have been indoctrinated are driving what we think and do. So how can we set about changing these beliefs?

Flying on automatic pilot

Well, the first thing we have to do is become aware of just how often we are flying on automatic pilot. Once we are aware of this, we can remove the filters and begin to see things through our own reality and not that of others. We have to start owning our own experiences of life, rather than relying on previous conditioning.

For example, take a couple of Janet's experiences. As a child she loved singing and especially in church she would sing along to all the hymns at the top of her voice. Then one day somebody asked her to stop singing so loudly. She believed it was because she had a bad voice, and from that moment on stopped singing. The result? Today she believes she cannot sing in key.

She also enjoyed drawing and thought she was quite good at it. Then one day she drew a picture of some human intestines (it's not only small boys who have gruesome minds!) and the teacher scathingly held the drawing up so that the whole class could have a good laugh. The result? Today Janet believes she cannot draw.

But it doesn't have to stay like that. Once she had removed the filters — the thoughtless person in church who asked her to pipe down and the sarcastic schoolteacher — she was able to see that she was perfectly capable of singing in key if she wanted to, and, with a few lessons, could draw a passable picture. Life has intervened and she has chosen not to go back to either of these pursuits, but she now knows that she could if she wanted to. She is no longer flying on automatic pilot, but has taken over the controls and can now make her own choices.

What are some of the beliefs you have about yourself and where do you think you got them from? Try closing down your automatic pilot now and see what happens. Go on, you can do it!

Attitudes to material possessions

Raising children can also be an extremely costly and morally confusing business. Increasingly the victims of advertising, many young people today want more and more material things — the complete Barbie set, an X-Box, the latest computer. As they grow older, many are conditioned to want the latest gadgets. Their attitude to things is different from the days when most young people had to save up their pocket money to buy a bicycle, saved their wages to buy a second-hand car, worked hard to pay the mortgage on a house and often got married and had children young, struggling financially until, when in their forties, they became freer to enjoy the money they had accumulated.

Attitudes towards material possessions in 21st-century Western society change the equation and create a different discussion from days gone by. The children of previous generations played with fairly simple things and toys were as limited as the income of the family. But while financial resources were limited for the average family, time was not. The world was also not as competitive as it is today, so more fathers worked regular hours and could spend more time with their children than the average father does today.

The things children played with ranged from household objects such as pots and pans, plastic containers, sand, home-made play dough and cotton reels. Today children are product driven. The media gets young children hooked on programs and characters, so they begin at an early age to demand what is presented to them on the television.

Parents succumb for a number of reasons. Principal among these are:

- To keep children quiet
- To ensure they have the same toys as their friends
- To alleviate their guilt about being time poor
- Their belief that the more things children have, the smarter they will be
- They don't have energy to argue
- They are tired
- They are busy

Of course it is a privilege for us to be able to give our children material things. However, these can cause long-term harm if not managed properly in terms of children's attitudes, gratitude and sense of a shared world. Children need to learn that they cannot have everything they want. In this sense, expensive material items should be reserved for birthdays, Christmas or special moments in between. The withholding of instant gratification is an important lesson that children need to conquer and they need to be taught to have a healthy perspective on such things. Children will respect and look after something that they have saved up for or waited a long time to receive much more carefully than if they are used to being given everything they want on demand. This also teaches them a sense of appreciation, which in turn leads to them being more careful of other people's property.

The need for stimulation

It is true nevertheless that, from birth, children need to be stimulated. They need colourful objects to fire their imaginations. Older children need to experience more three-dimensional activities, as most pastimes they engage in these days are flat: reading, watching TV, playing computer games. Their depth of vision suffers and this in turn shuts down parts of the brain. When playing out of doors, their eyes are constantly having close and far vision practice, which activates the brain and is healthier than sitting in a closed room staring fixedly at a square screen.

Many of the activities children take part in today are passive — they sit and watch, or sit and play. These activities do not require the same responses from the child mentally that being up and about playing with things demand. When they are out playing, they are stimulating more of their tactile, sight and smell senses. This in turn demands a greater response from them, and encourages creativity.

Many parents choose their child's activities according to their learning potential. We discuss this issue in greater depth in Chapter 16 when we come to the importance of play and leisure time. Generally, activities such as music, tennis, ballet, cricket and little athletics only really succeed in robbing children of the time to play. Children on the whole will learn far more by staying home and just playing, be it on their own or with other children.

MANAGING YOUR TIME

Ask yourself this question: what is the most expensive commodity in your household today? The answer for most people is *time*!

Anyone in business knows that productive people manage their time well. This is particularly important when it comes to children. Often a major issue in homes where both parents work, time management needs to be a priority right from the beginning. Young children on the whole do not respond well to being rushed. They are pushed to hurry in the morning because parents need to get them to school so they can get themselves to work on time. Children are happy to sit and eat, play and think for ages, yet from quite an early age we expect them to be mini adults: eat their food at the speed we do and rush out of the house, often just to get to preschool care. It's hard for them to understand and does little for their wellbeing.

"There's little more you can do for your children than just spending time with them — any old time."

We don't agree with the notion that 'quality' time is superior to the quantity of time spent with children. It's rubbish! There's nothing better you can do for your children than just spending time with them — any old time. Now, we realise that this isn't always convenient, and people have to work. We cannot easily regulate when children need to be with us, but sometimes it is in just such a moment that their self-esteem can be diminished — when they really need us and we aren't there. Being available is important in any relationship.

In early-21st-century Western society, increasing numbers of children are cared for by nannies, or spend time in childcare centres or pre- or afterschool care, which obviously reduces the time they spend with their parents. If both parents work, then it is vital that there is a regular timetable in place when the children know that they can guarantee to see their mum and dad. There is nothing more unsettling for a child than not knowing when they are going to see their parents again, particularly for younger children.

Spending time with children should be a fun and rewarding experience for parents. The children benefit greatly too: during these times they discover and learn about people and how they interact and feel. Children feel enormously important when their parents give them their undivided attention with no ulterior motives and no resentment — it boosts their self-esteem and makes them feel wanted and loved.

This does not imply in any way that our lives should be ruled by our children. Nothing could be further from the truth. Ideally, though, you should endeavour to spend as much time as is physically possible with your child. You will reap the benefits later in life.

7

building
your child's
self-esteem

Children need unconditional love, which is loving a person even when they are unlovable. It is when our children are difficult that they need to feel love most of all. If Johnny receives kisses and accolades when he does well at school and criticism when he fails, he gets the message that he is only loved if and when he does well. Children need to know they are loved even when they are not doing well.

Children with low self-esteem typically focus on trying to prove themselves or impress others. Some act with arrogance and contempt towards others to hide their lack of confidence in themselves, and often have doubts about their worth and acceptability, hence are reluctant to take risks or expose themselves to failure. They frequently blame others for their shortcomings rather than take responsibility for their actions.

A close relationship has been documented between low self-esteem and future social problems such as violence, alcoholism, drug abuse, eating disorders, school dropouts, teenage pregnancy, suicide, and low academic achievement.

However, it is critical that any efforts to build a child's self-esteem must be grounded in reality. Heaping children with undeserved praise that is not based on real accomplishment, for example, will not be successful. Self-esteem cannot be attained by merely reciting boosters or affirmations, such as 'You are a worthwhile person.' This will not encourage authentic self-esteem, but is more likely to result in an inflated and confusing sense of worth. It is generally believed that a sense of competence is strengthened more through realistic and accurate self-appraisal, meaningful accomplishments, overcoming adversities and bouncing back from failures. These are the things that give the child a true feeling of self-worth and it is here that we can best help the child grow and mature.

THE BUILDING BLOCKS

Self-esteem is the end result of a healthy relationship between a child and their world. There are many things you can do to build self-esteem in your children; we liken it to building blocks as a firm foundation to a house. By raising this deliberately into your consciousness on a daily basis, you will effectively build a firm foundation. Let's start with three building blocks.

1. Make your child feel special

To make your child feel special, consider and appreciate what is unique about them. You may have several children — what will work for one may not for another. Be creative and understanding as you treat each child as a unique and wonderful human being. Never miss an opportunity to tell your children how special they are and how lucky you are to have them. Tell them all the things you like about them.

When you have a moment, jot down on a piece of paper five characteristics about your child that are unique. Some parents may find this quite difficult, particularly if you have been finding your child's behaviour challenging.

Having completed your list of five unique characteristics, the next step is to begin *telling* your child all the wonderful, unique things about them.

For example, if you have written down that Justine is a very loyal friend, when you notice this happening, say to her something like: 'Justine, you really are a very loyal person. What you did for Jenny today is so special.' You can reinforce this by telling other people, so that your child regularly hears that you appreciate their uniqueness.

2. Show love and affection

Showing love and affection in a variety of ways allows children to be comfortable with intimacy and physical affection. At this point you may be thinking to yourself, I already do that! Great! However, sometimes we take our loved ones, including our children, for granted. We want to raise your level of awareness of this possibility, so let's be really honest and ask ourselves:

- Do I give affection to my daughter when she is being quiet?
- Do I wave to my son when he is playing happily?
- Do I spontaneously give my child a hug?

Think of the many ways you can demonstrate affection. These might include a smile, a hug, a wink, patting, tickling, thumbs up, or high fives. By concentrating on the feel-good stuff and letting go of the negatives, you will find the inappropriate and attention-seeking behaviour decreasing rapidly. This is guaranteed!

Children love our attention and sometimes when we are busy on the telephone, peeling the vegies, ironing, washing up or attending to other household tasks, we tend to be focused on that task and find it difficult to stop for a moment and give our child attention. Children will feel special if you stop the ironing for one minute to look at the special drawing or Lego construction they have just made.

Steve, a dad attending one of our workshops, volunteered to take on a role-playing exercise. He played the busy father, not able to give attention to his child. He was talking on his mobile and ignored the child showing him her drawing. In the replay, to demonstrate really attending to his child, he finished the phone call and gave her attention. When asked how he felt the second time, he answered quite spontaneously, 'Empowered.'

Naturally parents cannot stop every phone conversation whenever a child interrupts, but we can sometimes pause in the middle of our business to spend a few moments to attend.

3. Give your child choices

Giving choices in many different situations is another way of empowering children and helping them feel they are special and that their opinions are important. Often misbehaviour stems from a child feeling powerless.

Toddlers and younger children may have to have rather limited choices, such as 'What would you like to eat, a banana or an apple?'

Consider ways you can give your child a choice about their daily routines. You could offer your five-year-old the choice of what to wear to preschool or to a party, a four-year-old the choice of what Dad will cook for dinner on Wednesday nights. A six-year-old may be given the choice of taking their shower before or after dinner.

RESPECTING YOUR CHILD

It is equally important that your child is treated with empathy and understanding, and feels respected. This requires the ability to listen to your child, to be open to new possibilities and to have the courage to change your thinking.

Respect has to be earned. It is earned when we treat our children with the same respect we require from them, even when they are exhibiting challenging behaviour. Saying something like 'Don't yell at me, you brat!' or 'Stop crying or I'll smack you!' does not evoke respect. Respect enables children to grow in confidence.

When children feel and know that they are heard and their opinions are respected, then inappropriate, attention-seeking behaviour decreases, as confidence and self-assurance grows. If they feel that they are not being heard then situations like the following may occur.

Seven-year-old Freddy was being bullied in the playground, but was unable to talk about it with his parents or teacher. He did not feel he was being heard, because every time he spoke to his parents about it they said he was being silly. It was only when he took a knife to school for protection that his parents realised there was a serious problem.

Use positive language

Language can be used as a tool to show and teach respect. Positive language involves phrasing language into a positive rather than a negative framework, and using it at all times. This can be hard for busy parents and teachers.

It is useful to take a few moments to consider the undesirable behaviour, turn it around into the desired or preferred behaviour, and clearly state what you want your child to do rather than what you do not want.

For example, Susie is running through the house and her mum wants her to walk. Her mum may shout: 'How many times do I have to tell you? No running in the house!' It is far more respectful to say, 'Remember to walk inside please, Susie.'

Separate the child from the behaviour

Try never to label your children as naughty or stupid — rather, separate them from the inappropriate behaviour. So, for example, you may say, 'Hitting is not OK, Dad does not like hitting.' This clearly demonstrates that it is the *hitting* you do not like. Remember, we need to respect our children even when the behaviour is challenging! This is not easy, but very important to keep your child's self-esteem intact.

We explore the importance of positive language in greater depth in Chapter 10.

Body language

Body language is another powerful tool you can use to demonstrate respect for your child. Positive uses of body language include giving close attention to what a child wants to show you, physically getting down to their level, and making eye contact at all times.

Sarah comes running into the kitchen while her dad is washing up, indicating that she wants to show him her drawing. Her dad keeps on washing up and says, 'That's nice.' There are two problems with this response: 'nice' is a nothing word, so it tells her nothing; and the fact that he did not stop and give her his full attention gives Sarah the message that she and/or what she is doing is not important enough for him to stop what he is doing for one moment. Remember Steve, our workshop dad, and how empowered he felt when he took time to really listen?

Be a role model

Children love to mimic adults, so acting as a role model is a wonderful way to teach respect and empathy. Terry complained that he could not get two-year-old Jack to wear a hat outdoors. However, Terry didn't wear *his* hat outdoors, so why would

Jack want to wear one? Two-year-olds are great mimics. He wants to be like Dad, so if Dad wants Jack to wear a hat, he must make a point of putting one on his own head first!

Be consistent

Consistency is another method you can use to demonstrate that you respect your child. Two ways to do this are:

- Never give in
- Think before saying 'no'

It is important to take a few seconds to think about what your child is asking before you say 'no'. If you say 'no' because you are busy or distracted, then change your answer to 'yes', you are setting yourself up for the dreaded nagging! They have learned that you may change your mind.

Make time

Another building block of self-esteem is making time for your child every day. Setting aside a special time to talk about their day provides a safe place to share triumphs, trials, celebrations and disappointments. In an ideal world, try to give this time to each child individually. It may be at bedtime as you settle them down for sleep. Talk about your day too, sharing the highs and the lows. If your child knows there is this special time, they will look forward to it each day. This is guaranteed to diminish inappropriate attention-seeking behaviour.

Listen to your child

The simple act of listening, another important part of language and communication, will also build respect. Make time each day to *really* listen to your child. If you do that, their cup will be full to overflowing.

"Make time each day to really listen to your child."

Many parents ask the same old questions of their children and their partners: 'How was your day?' This sort of closed question more often than not receives only a monosyllabic answer: 'Good.' It is far more empathetic to ask open-ended questions, such as 'What was the best part of your day today?' or 'What did you think of your new teacher?'

This will also engage the limbic part of the brain — remember Dolphin Daisy from Chapter 3?

Using reflective language shows that you are listening. Peter may say, 'I felt frightened because the teacher yelled at me today.' 'Why did the teacher yell at you?' you might reply. Then this child will feel heard, as opposed to the parent who comes back with, 'My teacher used to yell at me too and . . .'

HAVE FUN WITH YOUR CHILD

Being involved with your child's preferred activities each day will help them feel valued and will foster a positive relationship. It is useful to ask yourself what your intention is when playing with your child. Parents usually answer, 'To have fun', 'To bond with my child', 'To see what they are interested in', and similar replies. However, if your intention is to teach your child something, or for them to learn something, it is not a child-preferred activity.

Paul came home early every afternoon to 'play' with his five-year-old daughter, Mia. He complained that she was taking up to an hour each evening to complete her meal and there was no time left to play. It turned out he was playing 'schools' — doing sums and becoming upset with Mia when she got her sums wrong.

This is not engaging in a child-preferred activity. All children love to play schools and, of course, delight in being the teacher and bossing you around. The sums and letters have very little to do with the game.

So, the moral of this story is to have fun — let your child lead the game.

EMPATHY

Acknowledging feelings and creating empathy will also support your child in feeling valued. Empathy is the ability to see things from the perspective of others. It requires refraining from prejudging what they need and opening up to what their interests and needs are.

By validating your child's verbal expression of feelings, you demonstrate that you acknowledge, respect and appreciate how they are feeling. This immediately lightens the burden of the emotion and acknowledges that feeling and emotions are normal for everyone. The aim is to teach children how to deal with feelings appropriately. We discuss feelings in more detail in Chapter 12.

FIVE WAYS TO MAKE YOUR CHILD FEEL VALUED

Children feel valued if they are encouraged and acknowledged for their efforts. Here are some easy ways in which you can make your child feel valued:

1. Spend frequent, brief amounts of time with them every day (as little as one or two minutes looking at a leaf, a butterfly or a drawing, for example).

2. Provide opportunities for quality time and conversations with them every day.

3. Be involved in child-preferred activities every day.

4. Acknowledge their feelings every day.

5. Give them encouragement every day.

While the home is the most important place to build self-esteem, it is vital that we establish open communication and partnerships with teachers and carers who also share and appreciate the importance of fostering self-esteem.

We have a burning desire to raise a generation of children who will have high self-esteem, be happy, love life and find learning easy and pleasurable. To achieve this, we need to attend to the business of building healthy relationships with them and, in so doing, nurturing healthy self-esteem.

8

nurturing your child's spirit

Young children are extremely vulnerable, so special care needs to be taken to nurture their spirit. Violating a child's spirit can occur in such a subtle way that often we do not realise what is happening. It occurs whenever the self-esteem of the child is eroded in any way, either through fear, anxiety or frustration.

What is self-esteem? As we discussed in the previous chapter, it is a feeling of equality with those around you, a feeling that you can cope in most situations, that you feel confident, have a good sense of self-worth, and can voice your opinions without fear of being ridiculed.

Here are some of the ways in which this self-esteem can be violated. This section is not intended to show you up as a bad parent, but will hopefully demonstrate just how easy it is to damage a child's spirit by accident.

VIOLATING A CHILD'S SPIRIT

As we have said before, our children don't come with instruction manuals, so it is left to us to do the best we can. Nobody sets out to deliberately do their child harm, but with children's brains being the complicated pieces of machinery that they are, harm can quite easily be done without realising it. Be honest with yourself as you read the following text, understand where you may be doing harmful things unintentionally and see if you can try a different approach.

There are three basic forms of violation of a child's spirit: physical, emotional and social.

1. Physical violations

Apart from the obvious cases of sexual and physical abuse, it is also possible to harm their spirit by grabbing their arms too tightly, or shouting at them, pinching them, pushing them or bullying them in any way. Every time we lose our temper with a child and shout at them, we are doing them harm. Unless this is quickly balanced with a hug or a kiss to show the child it is a momentary thing and that they are still loved, then it can have far-reaching effects.

Do you shout at your children? Of course you do — we all shout at some time or other, whether it's at our children or in other adult relationships. But do you make a point of showing them soon after that they are still loved and wanted? More importantly, perhaps, do you also admit that you were wrong to shout at them and apologise? This is an important lesson to teach children — that it is OK to be wrong, but we have to take responsibility for our behaviour and admit it when we are wrong.

2. Emotional violations

Emotional violations include criticising children, putting them down, teasing them, constantly correcting them, verbally bullying them or simply laughing at them.

Criticism

Criticism is a real esteem-sapper for children. Often it can be simple throwaway lines such as 'You're always the last to get in the car', 'Why can't you be like your sister? She always helps me with the washing up' or 'You're doing it all wrong, you silly-billy — watch me.' This all sounds harmless enough, but it can have an impact on a young mind.

Putting children down

Likewise, it is easy to put a child down with remarks such as 'You are so slow' or 'Come on, fatty — only joking!'

Teasing

Teasing is another way in which you can seriously damage a child's self-esteem. Avoid obvious expressions such as 'fatty', 'silly-billy', 'nerd' and similar terms, and teasing a young child about having a girl/boyfriend can be equally damaging. It may all seem like a bit of fun, and in some cases it is no more than that, but without realising it you could be doing more damage than you think. It is better to avoid such behaviour altogether.

Constant correction

Constant correction is another no-no. 'Pull your socks up', 'Hold your fork properly', 'Of course the sky isn't purple' —

this kind of correction can invalidate children and leave them with feelings of worthlessness.

Ridiculing

Equally damaging is laughing at children if they come out with a funny hairstyle or they've put their shoes on the wrong feet. They have tried to dress themselves and all they get in return is someone ridiculing them. The message they receive is: 'Look at me, aren't I silly, I can't even dress myself properly.'

3. Social violations

A child can be socially violated by being excluded from activities in which siblings or peers participate, being bullied at home or at school, having other children gang up against them, being gossiped about or being called names. All of these actions can have a devastating effect on a young child — indeed human beings of any age — and should be avoided at all costs.

All the above violations contribute to the formation of a child's belief system, which will later turn into their values, which, in turn, will drive their behaviour and thoughts for most of the rest of their life. Consequently, if a child's spirit is not being nurtured at an early age, then the very essence of the child's being feels squashed and crumpled.

Fundamental to the elimination and avoidance of these violations is understanding your child's development — to ensure that, as parents, your expectations are not unrealistic. To expect an eight-month-old baby not to put everything in their mouth is unrealistic. To tell a two-year-old boy he must share his new toy with his sister is unrealistic. To tell a four-year-old girl, who has just drawn a beautiful picture of her house, that the sky is not purple is destroying the child's creativity and connection to the truth as she sees it. All these actions squash and crumple the spirit of the child.

Until they are about eight years old, children need to be encouraged to make mistakes. It facilitates learning. If a child is continually told, 'No, don't do it that way, you're stupid' or similar remarks, their self-image quickly becomes negative and they start to believe that they cannot do anything properly. Often the result of this is children at schools all over the world who think they are no good at maths, or drawing or sport, while back at home there are children believing they are inherently naughty and difficult. This is all due to negative conditioning squashing the child's spirit.

If children do not receive approval, positive reinforcement, praise and encouragement they may well go on to look for other, less desirable, ways to win approval. Thus the class clown is born and becomes every teacher's nightmare, before moving on to other, even more undesirable ways of attracting love and attention, such as street graffiti, gangs, promiscuity, crime and even suicide.

Of course, not every child who fails to receive positive reinforcement turns out like Adolf Hitler, any more than every young person who graffitis the Town Hall wall comes from an uncaring household. But it is becoming increasingly clear that there is a strong link between the way a child's spirit has been nurtured during the growing-up process and their behaviour as young adults. While relatively little research has been undertaken on this subject in Australia, the evidence in other parts of the world, principally America, is compelling that child abuse in all its forms and at all levels is a significant factor contributing to crime. According to US Department of Justice statistics in 1997, men and women serving time in the nation's prisons reported a higher incidence of abuse as children than the general population. More than 33.3 per cent of women in the nation's prisons and jails reported abuse as children, compared with 12 to 17 per cent for women in the general population. About 14 per cent of male inmates reported abuse as children, compared with 5 to 8 per cent of men in the general population.

According to Benjamin Wolman, a leading American psychologist who has studied the behavioural patterns of people with an antisocial personality disorder for over 50 years, antisocial behaviour is strongly linked to inadequate parenting and abusive childhood environments. He claims that inadequate guidance, lack of moral encouragement, and frequent exposure to pathological selfishness foster antisocial personality development in young people.[9]

Let's not get alarmist about this, however. This is the very worst end of the scale. But you can now see how a child's mental growth can be affected by the attitudes and behaviour of their parents, and become aware that, even subconsciously, we can do harm unless we are careful.

PREVENTING VIOLATION

So what should we be doing to prevent this happening? Here's a true story:

> Jimmy, aged three, was with his Uncle Ted at a bowling green one afternoon. He asked his uncle what the people were doing.
>
> 'They're playing bowls,' replied Uncle Ted.
>
> 'How do you play that game?' asked Jimmy.
>
> 'Well,' replied Ted, 'you see that little white ball? That's called a jack, and the players have to get the big black balls as close as possible to the jack.' Jimmy watched the next ball being played closely and exclaimed excitedly: 'Wow, that was close!' At that moment Jimmy's dad arrived on the scene.
>
> 'Come on, Jimmy, let's go. Bowls is a stupid game,' he said.

Jimmy had started taking an interest in the game through the guidance of his Uncle Ted. Having mastered the simple rules, he had become involved and obviously thought it pretty interesting. Then along came Dad to take him away, at the same time telling him what a stupid game it was. What message do you think young Jimmy received from this? You'd be right! So you see how easy it is to violate a child's spirit without meaning any harm.

Let's look again at the three main areas of violation, but this time to see how we can avoid them.

Avoiding physical violation

This one's pretty obvious. You don't sexually abuse your child, you don't hit them, you try to avoid grabbing them roughly, you don't pinch or push or bully them in any other way.

Avoiding emotional violation

Try to avoid criticising your child. If you want to correct something that your child has said or done (or not done!), sandwich the correction between two positives. For example, Cathy keeps dropping her jigsaw puzzle pieces on the ground and never picks them up. The conversation could go something like this: 'Cathy, you're terrific at doing jigsaw puzzles — do you think you could keep the pieces on the table? Otherwise they might get lost, and I'd like to see how quickly you can do the puzzle next time.'

> ## "Avoid teasing or criticising your child."

Never put your child down. Remarks like 'You take forever making a sandwich ... here, let me do it' could become 'Would you like me to help you by slicing the tomato while you spread the butter? You're doing a great job!'

Don't tease your child. Very few children like being teased and it hurts them. Rather than saying things like 'Oooh, look who's got a boyfriend!' to your eight-year-old daughter, which will embarrass her and belittle the friendship, say instead: 'Would you like to invite Johnny over for tea? You two seem to get on really well.'

Avoiding social violation

If you suspect that your child is being bullied, or excluded, called names or gossiped about, encourage them to articulate their feelings. Make time for them, listen hard to what they say and let them know that it is safe to talk about what is bothering them. One way of doing this is not to gloss over the difficult things that happen in your own life. It is perfectly OK to come home from work and tell the family that you were angry in the office because your computer crashed and you lost a lot of valuable data or that you were hurt when your sister forgot to wish you a happy birthday. Let your children see that everybody, even their parents, suffers from bad things from time to time and that it is all right to talk about them.

Finally, and perhaps most importantly, always give your child positive reinforcement, praise and encouragement. Encourage them to experiment and make mistakes — that is how they learn. *It is not necessary to correct the mistakes!* Always use positive language and let your child know that you approve of what they are trying to do. If the child displays certain behaviour or uses certain language you would rather they didn't, then be careful how you correct this. Remember the 'correction between two positives' rule and couch your admonishment in positive terms.

"Always give your child positive reinforcement, praise and encouragement."

Being a role model is an ideal way to 'correct' a child. For example, rather than nagging your child constantly for dropping litter, put your litter in the bin at the park yourself. They will see you doing it and generally catch on pretty quickly.

Then there's truthfully telling your friend over the phone, 'I am really too busy to meet you today for coffee' instead of being tempted to say, 'Sarah is not well today, I have to stay in and care for her.' Your child will mimic you and if they hear you regularly using those little white lies they will think it is OK to lie too!

Younger children frequently use grammatically incorrect English and say things like 'I finish tidying my room, Mum.' It's tempting for a parent to criticise the grammar by saying 'I have finished' to the child. Instead, try saying: 'That's great, Dominic, I can see you *have finished tidying your room*. You're a good helper.' This way you have demonstrated the correct grammar in a conversational and non-critical way.

A child's confidence is as delicate as a butterfly's wing. It doesn't take very much to damage it. The British author and journalist Malcolm Muggeridge, one of the wittiest writers of the 20th century, said it best with the title of his autobiography. *Tread Softly for You Tread on My Dreams*. We hope this chapter has given you some valuable insights into how to avoid treading on your child's dreams.

9

communicating effectively with your child

L earning how to communicate effectively with your child is one of the keys to successful parenting. Probably a child's greatest need is to be heard, and then, once heard, to be understood. Let's face it, isn't that what we all want?

Despite this, many of us have never been taught how to communicate effectively. We have had to learn it for ourselves, and it can be hard to do. Men and women have entirely different communication techniques — that's lesson one and needs to be understood from the start. When women talk, they want to be listened to and understood. Men, on the whole, aren't satisfied just listening. They want to fix the problem, help you or advise you on how to solve things. Most men have never been taught active listening techniques, which often makes it harder for them to hear what their children are really saying. The first step in effective communication is effective listening.

THE IMPORTANCE OF LISTENING

So what is active listening? Basically, there are four main parts to it: making eye contact, watching your body language, making 'being heard' gestures and waiting until the other person has stopped talking before you say anything.

Eye contact

When you are talking to your child, no matter how old they may be, come down to their size so that you can see into their eyes, or, as the 16th-century French poet Guillaume de Salluste du Bartas so romantically put it, 'These lovely lamps, these windows of the soul'. Only by looking into someone's eyes when you speak to them can you determine the true emotions behind the words and therefore respond appropriately — which is, after all, what effective communication is all about.

Body language

To be able to look directly at your child, you need to stop whatever it is you are doing and pay them full attention. For a child to feel they are being heard, they need to feel that they are being attended to. Trying to continue with the cooking or washing while they try to explain to you why they have had such a lousy day at school will only give the impression that you don't really care, as will more subtle covert body language such as crossing your arms or affecting an impatient stance.

Put yourself in this scenario: you are trying to tell a friend something really important to you and in the middle of it their telephone rings, they leave you to take the call then talk for a quarter of an hour to someone else. How would you feel? Angry? Frustrated? Ignored? Unimportant? Probably all of those things and you would be justified. Your children will feel exactly the same. On the other hand, if your friend were to say, 'I'm sorry, I really want to hear what you are telling me, so just hang on one minute and I'll see who that is and get them to call back', how would you feel then? Special? Important? Valued? Respected? All of those things.

'Being heard' gestures

Having made eye contact with your child, you need to show that you are paying attention by nodding from time to time while they are speaking and showing appropriate facial expressions. You aren't going to do much for your child's self-esteem if they are telling you about how they are emotionally hurting and you start laughing! A more appropriate gesture would be to touch them lightly on the arm and make a sympathetic noise.

Waiting before speaking

The next time you are in a coffee shop and see a group of friends talking around a table, watch what happens. One person will start talking and before they have finished someone else has their mouth open ready to speak, often jumping in before the first person has finished their sentence. Go on, try it. You'll be amazed how often it happens. Active listening is the art of listening to someone for the purpose of understanding what they are saying. It is not about giving your opinion — that can come later if it is asked for. All your child generally wants is to be heard.

COMMUNICATING CLEARLY

Once you've mastered the art of active listening, you need to work on expressing yourself clearly. More relationship breakdowns result from unclear communication than any other cause, and that includes both parent–parent and parent–child relationships.

Often we will think something and then, when trying to impart that thought to the child, either end up not saying exactly what it is we were thinking or, alternatively, putting it in language that confuses the child. Then we become cross when the child fails to understand. Children are not mind readers. For them to understand, you have to be crystal-clear in what you are saying to them. At the same time, you must say what you are thinking. Often we have meant to say something, and think we have, but in the end forget to say it out loud!

Never assume that children understand anything. As someone once wisely said, 'To assume merely makes an ass out of u and me!' Assumption is the death of communication. When Janet was a fairly new kindergarten teacher, she said to her class one day: 'It's time to go home now. Everyone go and get your bags.' All the children went out, got their bags and returned to the classroom, except for little Brett. He took himself off home on his own as that was the instruction he had heard. Janet assumed she was being clear; Brett heard differently. The next time, Janet said, 'Everyone go and get your bags and bring them back here to the classroom.' Then, when everyone had returned, she told them that it was time

125

to go out and find Mum or Dad as it was time to go home. There is always another way to express things — and clarity is a must, especially with young children.

To ensure that your child has understood what you are saying, ask them to repeat it back to you. It's also advisable to ask them to do just one thing at a time — they can't take in much more than this.

> *"To ensure that your child has understood what you are saying, ask them to repeat it back to you."*

Appropriate language

Clear expression is aided by the use of appropriate language. Appropriate language means using language a child understands and giving them instructions in a way they will comprehend. For example, you are talking to a six-year-old girl and you want her to stop kicking the cat: 'Samantha, please desist from putting the boot into Fifi, she is only a small feline and your continual punishment will certainly do damage to her entrails.'

OK, we know this is a bit over the top, but can you see the point? A better way to put it would be simply to say: 'Samantha, please play gently with the cat, otherwise you will hurt her.'

There's no point in using the same sort of language with a six-year-old that you would use with a teenager or an adult. How often have you witnessed scenes in supermarkets with mothers of two-year-olds trying to explain in ten-year-old language why the child shouldn't be doing something or other. Of course the child doesn't listen, because, for a start, there have been far too many words to listen to and they have missed most of them, and, secondly, it is too difficult to respond to that kind of tirade at the age of two. In this instance, the two-year-old needs to be spoken to in short, clear sentences. That doesn't mean baby talk, mind you. That's equally inappropriate.

The other secret of good communication with children is telling them what you want them to do, not what they have done wrong. If a young child's room is messy and you want them to clean it up, rather than saying, 'Your room is always so messy', say to them clearly, 'Please tidy up your room and put all your clothes away in the cupboard.' Remember to use appropriate language, too. It's better not to say, 'Please clean up your room', which has a whole host of meanings — do you want them to take a bucket and cloth to the floor? A vacuum cleaner to the carpet?

By saying, 'Your hair is looking so untidy' you mean 'Please comb your hair.' 'Your school shoes are dirty' means 'Please clean your shoes.'

It's a matter of being simple and clear. Here are some more common sentences you might like to consider putting differently in future:

- 'You are very noisy in the car' might become 'I find it easier to drive safely when you are quiet in the car.'

- 'Don't run in the house' might become 'Please walk when you're in the house.'
- 'You never listen to a word I say' might become 'It makes me really happy when you listen to what I say.'

The positive approach is always more successful than the negative one. And, since the goal of communication is to state what we feel clearly, listen and get an outcome that is satisfactory to both parties, it is imperative to ensure that the person with whom we are communicating feels OK about themselves and that we have not in any way destroyed their confidence or self-esteem. This takes practice.

CONSIDER YOUR CHILD'S FEELINGS

As we discussed in Chapter 7, both confidence and self-esteem are delicate flowers in the hands of young children and need to be nurtured carefully. In communicating with a child you must always consider the child's feelings. Some parents have a tendency to talk about their children in front of them as though they are not there. The child squirms visibly but on ploughs the parent, oblivious to the harm being done to their child's self-esteem. So communication, even with children, must be done respectfully.

Let's take the room-tidying example again. How do you think a child feels if the parent says, 'You always do such and such' or 'You never do so and so'? Of course they feel that they have been judged and categorised, and that is that. They may be hurt by it, or they may simply not care, but, either way, they feel they have been condemned. If, on the other hand, we simply ask them to 'Please tidy up your room', there is no emotion or value judgment involved. The child may or may not choose to respond, but they do not feel put down. They still feel OK about themselves.

It's easy to put a dent in a child's self-worth without meaning to. In one family we know the parents gave a lot of attention to their daughter who behaved perfectly and achieved top academic results. The little girl's sister started calling her 'the preferred child' — not within the family, but outside the home — and it was years before the parents realised they had damaged their other daughter's self-esteem. How could they have avoided this? Simply by praising and giving attention to both daughters equally, acknowledging each for their uniqueness rather than expecting the two of them to be the same.

THE FIVE STYLES OF COMMUNICATION

There are five general styles of communication: non-assertive or passive; aggressive; passive–aggressive; manipulative; and assertive. Let's look at each of these as we might behave towards our children.

Non-assertive or passive

Our body language is hesitant and we don't make eye contact with the child. We adopt a begging voice and say things like 'It's my fault' or 'I'm sorry.' The message we are sending out is that their needs are more important than ours. The more children hear this message, the more they take it to heart and will ultimately end up treating their parents as worthless.

Aggressive

We use loud, demanding, abrasive language. We try to convince the child that only our way is right; we see any compromise as a weakness and will try to intimidate the child into doing what we want. The language we use might include statements like 'You never . . .', 'What is the matter with you?', 'It's all your fault', 'Do as you're told', 'Do it this way' or 'You are doing that all wrong — this is the way to do it.' This is a protective mechanism. By blaming the child, you may be covering up for your own feelings of inadequacy. The message that children hear from this is that the parents' needs are more important than their own.

Passive–aggressive

We moan and complain a lot about what is lacking, often using sarcasm or misdirected humour (usually making fun of the child), and only hint at what we want rather than being clear in the hope that the child will understand. Parents who are passive–aggressive rarely get their needs met because they don't successfully communicate their message, and their behaviour generally leaves their children confused, angry and resentful. Sulking is another type of passive–aggressive behaviour.

Manipulative

In this mode, we tend to play the role of either martyr or victim. The idea is to make the child feel sorry for us and, in some cases, we want the child to take care of us rather than the other way around. If this doesn't work, we will pretend not to care or become angry.

Assertive

Ideally this is the style we want to be working towards. Assertiveness is a combination of all the communication skills discussed in this chapter and tells the child that your needs and theirs are of equal importance. If your communications are assertive and non-aggressive, everybody involved has a greater feeling of self-worth, self-esteem and self-confidence.

SIX WAYS IN WHICH WE CAN COMMUNICATE BETTER

1. First, really listen to what your child is saying without formulating an opinion or making a judgment. Just stay in neutral. Then listen to the emotions behind your child's talk and respond appropriately without trying to solve or teach anything.

2. Recognise your children frequently by stopping to play a little game with them or sitting down to do a drawing. It need only last two minutes and they do appreciate it! **This is a powerful tool, guaranteed to cut down on whining and demanding behaviour.**

3. Take time to tell your children stories. Children love stories, especially true ones about Mummy and Daddy. It is a great way to open the lines of communication.

4. As your children grow older, encourage them to think for themselves by not immediately rushing to solve every problem. Ask them how they might solve it first.

5. Always tell children the truth. If you lie to them and they find out, the damage done is far greater than in the same situation with an adult. If you want a child to communicate openly with you, then you must be open with them. Children are brighter than you think!

6. Ask them what they are feeling and ask for their opinions. This is how children learn to form opinions and express feelings, and at the same time come to believe that their opinions are worth something.

10

communicating through language

Communication through language is a combination of a number of different actions: words, tone, expression and body language. For a child to understand what they are being told, all these actions need to be authentic, otherwise the message the child receives may not be clear.

Of course, the words we use with children change as they grow older. Language needs to be appropriate both to the age of the child and the situation in question. There's no point in using words such as 'proposition' with a two-year-old, whereas you'd expect that by the time the child has reached ten or twelve this word has some meaning.

Here's a story about a family we know. Candice had been trying for some time to persuade her husband, David, that he was using entirely inappropriate language with their two-year-old daughter Eliza. David disagreed, saying that the child should hear the correct words from an early age. It was a losing battle, until one day when David said to his daughter: 'Eliza, I have a proposition for you. If you pick up all these toys now you can have a biscuit.' Some hours later Eliza came to her dad and asked, 'Can I have another proposition please?' and later again that day, 'Can we take a proposition to the park, Daddy?' Finally, Dad learned the lesson.

We need to be very careful about the language we use with children, especially younger ones. Language can be loaded with innuendo, often totally unintended by the user, but picked up on by the child and wrongly interpreted.

TALK, TALK, TALK

The business of language starts right from birth. The words we use when cooing over the newborn, and go on to use as they grow into toddlers, form the basis of their vocabulary — and not only the words, but the looks and expressions that go with them. A baby that is spoken to very little will have a limited vocabulary; a baby spoken to often will learn much faster and strive to mimic the parents. In the Western world at least, most babies start off by saying 'Mama' and 'Dada', and then progress to 'no'. The typical two-year-old has a vocabulary of more than 150 words.

The age at which children begin using language ranges widely, and anxious parents of late talkers are regularly told not to worry. There is a story that the great evolutionary scientist Charles Darwin never uttered a word until he was seven years old. One day he was out walking with his mother, who would talk away to him without expecting any reply. 'Come on, darling, let's go down this road,' she said. At this point Darwin reputedly uttered the first words of his life: 'That's not a road, Mummy, that's a path!'

Why Won't My Child Listen?

However, recent findings from a long-running study conducted by Dr Leslie Rescorla, chair of the Department of Psychology at Bryn Mawr College, Pennsylvania, and director of the school's Child Study Institute, show that children who are slow to begin talking often continue to have weakness in language-related skills for years, even if they seem to catch up with their peers by the time they enter school. Late talkers may subtly lag in vocabulary, grammar, reading and spelling as they progress through school.

According to Dr Rescorla, the 'don't worry' approach is not unusual when it comes to late talkers, especially when the child appears to be on target for other developmental milestones. She says parents of a late-talking child will sometimes joke, 'She'll talk when she has something to say' or 'He doesn't have to talk; his big sister does it for him.' However, she doesn't think parents of an otherwise normal child should hit the panic button if there isn't much vocabulary by the age of two. If there's little progress by two and a half, then an evaluation is a good idea.[10]

Words are what give children their earliest sense of identity, and the more you talk to them, the more they are likely to respond. This is how they start making sense of their world. Parents who insist on correcting small children who are just starting to speak run the risk of making them afraid to try. The important thing at this stage is that they are learning to use language, not that their grammar or even word usage is correct. However, you might be surprised at what they understand!

Reading to your child from an early age is also an important way of introducing them to words. Reading should be done purely for its own sake, with the aim of encouraging a love of books in the child. It shouldn't ever be used as a teaching or testing aid, but simply to foster the love and enjoyment of reading. Leave the testing to school!

"Words are what give children their earliest sense of identity, and the more you talk to them, the more they are likely to respond."

Children are never too old to be read to, and once they can read for themselves, it doesn't mean you should stop reading to them. Apart from being able to introduce them to more advanced concepts in this way, it also helps them with their auditory sense of words, quite apart from the obvious advantages of the bonding experience. We recommend that you read to your child for as long as they are willing to let you.

LITTLE LOGIC!

At this early age children tend to think very logically and, as a result, can come up with some hilarious ideas. One example is six-year-old Jeremy, whose teacher was reading the story of the Three Little Pigs to her preschool class. She came to the part in the story where the first pig was trying to gather the building materials for his home.

She read, '. . . and so the pig went up to the man with the wheelbarrow full of straw and said, "Pardon me, sir, but may I have some of that straw to build my house?"'

The teacher paused, then asked the class, 'And what do you think the man said to the little pig?'

Jeremy raised his hand and replied, very matter-of-factly, 'I think the man would have said, "Well, bugger me, a talking pig!"'

The teacher was unable to teach for the next ten minutes, so hard was she laughing.

THE 'NO' WORD

We have established that a small child's earliest language attempt is likely to contain the simple word 'no'. As the child grows and develops, 'no' will remain with them and probably become more and more frequent. Parents need to be careful how they use this word — if they want it to have any real meaning to the child, then they must avoid using it over and over again until it loses its meaning. Coupled with 'no' is that other favourite parental admonishment, 'don't'. Like 'no', if 'don't' is overused, it too will soon lose its meaning.

'Don't do that or Mummy will have to smack you!'

Mummy has never smacked the child. Mummy has no intention of ever smacking her child. The child soon learns that Mummy isn't going to smack them at all so learns that the word 'don't' isn't really a serious word, and consequently never responds to it.

THE FIVE RULES OF LANGUAGE

The following are five rules for using appropriate language with a small child.

1. Say only what you mean

Saying 'no' and 'don't' can almost become reflex actions if we aren't careful. Before you use either of these words, see if you can stop and ask yourself this question: 'Do I really mean it?' Unless you are absolutely positive that you want your child to stop doing whatever it is, then don't stop them. If you mean it, then say it in an absolutely clear and firm voice. It won't take long for them to learn what behaviour is acceptable to you and what is out of bounds. For example, they may be playing with your purse. You don't really mind, but you have noticed that at playgroup the other mothers feel that it is wrong for children to play with purses. So you say 'no' to your child, but in your heart of hearts you don't really care if they do. This half-heartedness effectively undermines the authority that you muster when you really *don't* want them to do something, and they very quickly pick up on that. 'Stop!' is a very effective word. It is short, sharp and to the point — telling the child exactly what you want them to do.

2. Sort out what's important

If you say 'no' to every little thing that an inquisitive toddler does, you'd never have the time of day to say or do anything else! Ask yourself, 'Does it really matter?' If it doesn't, then say nothing. Effective parenting is planned and thought out. Are you saying 'no' because you are on automatic pilot or because your mother, or your neighbour, or Aunt Jemima in South Africa thinks it's wrong? Or are you saying 'no' because you have thought the action through and decided that the issue is worth making a definite stand on?

3. Explain WHY

If an issue is worth making a fuss about, there is another important component — and that is saying *why* you want your child to do, or stop doing, something.

Instead of saying, 'Don't touch that vase!', think about *why* you don't want the child to touch the object and reframe the sentence. For example: 'That vase can break easily, so we'd better not touch it' or 'The stove is hot and you might get burnt if you touch it.' No doubt you can think of many more different ways in which you can be clearer when giving your child instructions. It is not necessary at this stage to elaborate on the reasons why you don't want the child to do something — the fact that the stove is hot and they may burn themselves is sufficient. (Why the stove is hot and how electricity works is best left for another time!)

As mentioned previously, the language we use needs to be appropriate to the age of the child. A two-year-old has a simple vocabulary and can only respond to short, simple instructions. As children grow older, you can start introducing more complicated ideas, but never find yourself in the position where, when you have said 'no' and then been asked 'why?', you reply, 'Because I said so.' That is like a red rag to a bull with young children. They want to know why, and if you want to be effective, you need to tell them why. At this young age they require enough information to satisfy their curiosity and see your point of view.

As they grow older still, they will, at times, not see your logic at all and will disagree. Again, saying 'Because I said so' will not be successful. Instead you might try saying something like 'I can see your point of view, but we need to do it my way because we don't have time to discuss yours right now.'

4. Never threaten or make instructions conditional

Statements like 'If you don't stop doing that, I won't let you have an ice-cream' are manipulative and should be avoided. Statements such as 'If you eat all your food up, I'll give you an ice-cream' are conditional and should also be avoided. Why? Because if you want a child to do something, you need to tell them simply and clearly. No ifs and buts. Children understand straight talking and often don't respond very well to threats or conditions. Do you?

5. Always follow through

When you say you are going to do something, *do it*! Idle threats will only undermine your authority in the long run and, like the little boy who cried wolf, soon your child will stop listening to you.

'The next time you hit your brother, I'll take your PlayStation away.'

Wham! Brother gets another wallop. 'I've warned you. The next time I take your PlayStation.' Ouch! A sly kick this time. 'Listen, Peter, how many times do I have to say it? Stop hitting your brother or you'll lose your PlayStation.'

Sorry, but that simply won't work. Try this instead. 'Peter, remember our rule is to play gently. Next time you forget this rule you will have no PlayStation for the rest of the day.' Wham! Brother gets another wallop. 'OK, that's it. No PlayStation until tomorrow.' This way the child knows you mean business and will respect future instructions, realising that there are immediate consequences for forgetting (or ignoring) the rules.

Parents often feel that they are being too hard on their children by using this sort of instant retribution, but believe us, you're not being hard, you're being *clear and consistent*. Your children will appreciate it. We will cover this further when we discuss boundaries and limits in Chapter 15.

CHOOSE YOUR WORDS CAREFULLY

You might not realise it, but the actual words you use have a huge impact on a child's self-esteem. There are certain words we advise you to eradicate from your vocabulary immediately. The three most important are 'naughty', 'bad' and 'wrong'.

When children are told they are any of these three, they immediately attach the word to their perception of themselves. They feel condemned by them and will most likely behave accordingly: 'If they think I'm naughty, I might as well be naughty.' If you must use these words, then attach them to the act or behaviour, *not* to the child: 'Hitting is naughty. Don't hit Sarah again', 'It's bad to tell lies — please tell the truth in future' or 'It is wrong to steal — give the money back.' Stating a fact does not erode self-esteem. 'You are naughty' is far more personal than 'Hitting is naughty.'

"Delete these words from your vocabulary: 'naughty', 'bad', 'wrong'."

'Good' and 'right' are two more words you would do well to drop from your vocabulary if you can. They may seem innocuous, but they are subtler in their damage. For example, if you say to your daughter, 'What a good girl you are', she will feel that she needs to keep doing things to get this type of praise. This may make you feel better, but doesn't really help when you remember that one of the main aims of effective parenting is to raise your children to become independent in their physical activities and their thinking. If they are continually told they are good or what they are doing is right, they will begin to lose their own voice and become people-pleasers, which may lead in later life to co-dependency and other relationship issues.

The common characteristics of co-dependency include a fear of rejection determining what they may say or do, their own hobbies and interests being put to one side in preference to sharing someone else's, any good feelings about themselves stemming from receiving approval from someone else, and putting their values aside in order to connect with the person they have become dependent upon.

Other relationship issues can include, for example, their ability to make good decisions. Every parent has known the tension of having to say 'no' to an activity their child desperately wanted to attend. A sleepover at a home where adult supervision will be lacking, attending a concert that may contain inappropriate material, wanting to take on one too many extracurricular activities — telling your children they cannot participate in any of these will lead to disappointment and even anger. Parents who are prone to people-pleasing will find themselves compromising their own good judgment just to keep their children happy. Being a people-pleaser can make people uncomfortable around you. An over-eager personality craves an inordinate amount of feedback. Every task, no matter how small, demands a response: 'Did I do this well?'

A spouse who needs constant affirmation because of their insecurity will slowly but surely stifle their marriage. An 'I love you' becomes not a declaration of affection but the prompt to hear the other say, 'I love you too.'

Many middle-aged men and women find themselves in therapy today because they feel they lost their uniqueness and personal style when young. They consequently feel trapped and suppressed as adults and this can often be traced back to the way their parents spoke to them as children.

Words need to encourage young children, not put them down. Phrases like 'I like it when . . .' or 'When you do that, it makes me happy' will build a child's self-esteem.

We know a family in which the two children, aged eight and ten, hardly ever get the chance to speak to their father. When he does speak to them, he tells them that they are naughty or wrong. So when he says, 'This place is a mess. You are both very naughty — put your toys away at once', they sulkily tidy up and give Dad a wide berth. Mum, on the other hand, doesn't use words such as 'no' and 'wrong' and 'bad'. When the place is in a mess, she says to the children: 'What a mess! Let's all get stuck in and see how quickly we can get it tidied and then we can all sit down and watch television together.' The children generally do what Mum asks them to, and they are open and frank with her because she builds their self-esteem and they feel positive around her.

So, the next time you open your mouth to say 'no' or start to admonish your child, stop for a second and think, Is there a better way of putting this?

11

communicating through the senses

In addition to verbal expression, another important means of communicating with a child is through their senses, particularly touch. By stimulating the tactile system, children grow to be in touch with their bodies and how their bodies feel. This, in turn, helps them become aware of their feelings and emotions. Then we can teach them how to express these emotions in appropriate and healthy ways.

The senses of touch, taste, hearing, smell and sight all need to be stimulated in young children, and you may have noticed, if your child goes to preschool, that early childhood carers use a variety of activities to stimulate the tactile system. You can do this yourself at home in many simple ways.

"Play is the best form of learning for young children."

For example, gather together a variety of objects that are rough and smooth, hard and soft, cold, wet or prickly. Babies and young children love touching things and testing them, frequently by trying to put them in their mouths, so that they can gain an idea of what they are holding. As the child grows older, you can offer many tactile experiences, such as water play, play dough, slime, shaving cream, finger paints, mud and sand play, and gardening. Without a doubt, play is the best form of learning for young children.

There is nothing a child likes better than to get dirty, rolling around in a sandpit or covering themselves with shaving cream or green slime. It's one of the best things you can let them do — it helps them towards a greater sense of freedom and wellbeing. Just make sure that they are wearing some appropriate clothes that you can drop into the washing machine at the end of the game, and there should be no trouble.

SOME IDEAS TO GET YOU STARTED

So, what can you do at home to stimulate the various senses? Here are a few ideas to get you started.

Stimulating touch

- Put two or three objects of different consistency in a small drawstring bag and see if the child can guess what they are just by feeling them. Ask the child to describe what they are feeling and how that makes them feel at the time. Ask them questions about their experiences, like 'Which was the softest?' or 'Which was the coldest?' This game also helps enhance their vocabulary.
- Let the child take off their shoes and socks and walk bare-foot on the grass, then on sand and then on gravel. Get them to describe the different feelings as they do it.

- At the end of a hot, tiring school day give your child a ten-minute body massage using either talcum powder or baby oil. Teach them how to relax and enjoy the feeling of being touched by another person.

Stimulating sight

- Ask your child to draw a picture of their day with coloured crayons. Most small children are innately artistic and this is a great way to expand their imagination, as well as giving parents valuable clues to how their child may be feeling at the time. For this reason, we would advise against colouring-in books. They tend to limit a child's imagination rather than let it expand naturally.
- Sit with your child and watch TV programs that are full of colour and movement. Both these stimulate the child's sense of sight and heighten their awareness. Make sure, of course, that the show is age appropriate.
- Take your child on a field expedition to the garden or park in search of flowers and insects, or to look at the birds.
- A treasure hunt is another good way of stimulating a child's sight sense, by making them find specific items such as a feather, or a small, round stone. Another advantage of this is that it helps to develop the child's three-dimensional vision by making them look at objects both in close proximity and further away, in a way that watching TV or playing computer games will not do as their vision becomes fixed on one spot.

Stimulating smell

Smell is possibly the most powerful of all the senses, and the association between certain smells and events or emotions will carry with the child right through their life.

- Let your children help you in the kitchen when you are cooking. Encourage them to smell the ingredients you are using and — being careful of course to avoid burns — let them smell the food as it comes out of the oven.
- 'Guess the smell' is a wonderful game for young children. Gather together about six or eight small plastic containers and fill them with everyday substances such as lemon, coffee, chocolate and Vegemite. Then blindfold the child and see if they can guess what the content of each container is.

Stimulating taste

- Give your child little tastes of different foods as you are cooking. Where appropriate, let them taste foodstuffs raw and then again after they have been cooked, so that your child can taste the difference.
- 'Guess the taste' is played in exactly the same way as 'Guess the smell', but let your child taste small amounts of each substance and see if they can pick it. Also encourage them to use descriptive words like 'sour' and 'sweet'.

In addition to exposing your child to all of these sensations, you will find it enormously helpful to determine what sort of

Why Won't My Child Listen?

a learner they are. We all have different ways of processing information and if you are trying to teach your child something and it isn't sinking in, you probably haven't cottoned on to the best way in which they absorb information.

THE THREE TYPES OF LEARNERS

Auditory

If they listen attentively to what you tell them then your child is principally an auditory learner. These are the children who tend to sit at the front of the class where they can hear well. They will have a tendency to hum or talk to themselves or others when bored, and they remember information best by verbalising lessons to themselves. Auditory learners acquire knowledge by reading aloud and may have difficulty with such tasks as reading to themselves, understanding diagrams or handling conceptual assignments such as mathematics. They are generally less competent at activities such as colour coordination — but if you ask them why they paired a pink dress with orange shoes, they will have a perfectly rational answer for you!

Visual

Visual learners, on the other hand, approach learning in quite a different way. They are usually very neat and clean and often close their eyes to visualise or remember something. They like to see what they are learning and benefit enormously from

152

illustrations and presentations that use lots of colour. If they are bored, they will search out something to look at and are attracted to written or spoken language that is rich in imagery. They learn better through looking at pictures.

Kinesthetic

The kinesthetic learner is a whole different type again. Their learning is governed by movement; they need to be active and take frequent breaks and tend to throw their hands around a lot when they speak. They can remember perfectly what they've been doing, but have difficulty recalling what was said or seen at the time. They are compulsive doers and enjoy getting out and about and taking part in activities that involve making things. They tend to become bored easily if there is no chance for hands-on experiences and can be very restless, wanting to get up and wander about a lot rather than sitting still for long periods of time. They communicate by touching, and appreciate physically expressed encouragement, such as a pat on the back.

How to pick your child's type

There is a range of ways in which you can determine what sort of a learner someone is, the best known of which is probably the Myer Briggs Type Indicator. The MBTI is a self-report questionnaire designed to make the theory of psychological types, as devised originally by the Swiss psychiatrist Carl Jung, understandable and useful in everyday life. Katharine Cook Briggs and her daughter, Isabel Briggs Myer, spent more than 50 years after World War II researching and developing the Indicator based on thousands of personal interviews. The process is, however, quite lengthy and ideally needs an accredited administrator to interpret the results.

But there is another, simple method that accords closely with our idea of dividing the childhood brain into different animal types, and that is the Herrmann Brain Dominance Instrument (HBDI).

Shortly after World War II, the giant General Electric company (GE) in America hired a psychologist, Ned Herrmann, to teach its employees how to become creative again and put GE back at the top of the innovative company league table. Herrmann came up with the HBDI, which basically classifies people in terms of their relative preferences for thinking. He reasoned that people basically thought in four different ways, based on the functioning of their physical brain.

In his theory, the four modes or quadrants in this classification are:

Quadrant A. Logical, analytical, quantitative, factual and critical

Quadrant B. Sequential, organised, planned, detailed and structured

Quadrant C. Emotional, interpersonal, sensory, kinesthetic and symbolic

Quadrant D. Visual, holistic and innovative [11]

You can determine into which category your child falls by using the examples in the three different learning types set out over the previous pages. If you have more than one child, it is likely that they will exhibit quite different learning styles, and this is where many parents have inadvertently become disheartened at the way their children respond to their attempts to interact with them. It is important, however, not to put your children in a box, or tell them that they are one particular type, for this will inhibit them breaking out and experimenting with different approaches.

Nevertheless, you can't expect a Front-Brain Foxy Fred and a Back-Brain Baboon Bertie to respond in the same way to your instructions, any more than the logical Left-Brain Larry Lion will react in the same way as the emotional Right-Brain Rhino Raymond.

Your life will become much simpler if you work out the best way to get each individual child to respond to you.

12

dealing with feelings

S trange as it may seem, we are all totally responsible for what we feel! Feelings don't just appear out of the blue and out of our control, they don't just *happen*. Sad or happy or angry feelings are the result of an interpretation that we have consciously or subconsciously made of a situation.

There is a definite order to feelings. It goes like this:

Event ⟶ Interpretation ⟶ Feeling

Here's an example:

The event: *You are driving in traffic when someone in the car behind pulls out and screeches around you to get in front, narrowly missing your front bumper.*

The interpretation: *'How dare they do that! I'm furious.'*

The feeling: *Anger and aggressiveness.*

But there is another way of interpreting that event and that is to say to yourself, 'Stupid idiot, he won't get there any faster in this traffic', and just shrug the whole thing off. The feeling resulting from that interpretation is likely to be one of calm and even wry humour.

Everyone's interpretation and subsequent feelings are different. Imagine you're at a party when a particular person walks into the room. You look at them with interest, which leads to a feeling of excitement. Someone next to you, unbeknown to you, is looking at the same person with disinterest, which may lead to a feeling of dislike; while a third person in the room has hardly noticed the new guest, regarding them with complete indifference and consequently has no feelings about the person whatsoever.

"We are all responsible for what we feel."

So you can see from these examples that the first step in becoming fully functioning and responsible human beings is to know what we are feeling at any given time. Believe it or not, many adults have great difficulty knowing what they are feeling, and children often have even less idea and certainly have great difficulty in expressing it.

THE SIX STEPS TO DEALING WITH FEELINGS

Our goal here is to teach our children to express their feelings safely and appropriately. They know exactly how they feel, even if they don't necessarily have a name for it, and often they don't know how to tell you about it. Here are six steps to help you deal with your child's feelings.

1. Acknowledge the feeling

The first step in the process is **acknowledging** their feelings. All this means is just noticing what they feel, that is, *feeling* the feeling and then naming it. Have you ever asked a person who is really angry what is making them so angry, and they deny it until they are blue in the face? They simply cannot acknowledge the fact that they feel angry. Children may not realise they are angry unless they are taught what being angry *feels* like.

For example, Tommy is hitting his sister. You can deal with this in two ways. One is by saying to him, 'Tommy, you are a naughty boy for hitting Susie.' The outcome of this approach is most likely that Tommy hears the negative message that he is naughty, but the rage or annoyance that he is feeling goes unacknowledged. In this case, Tommy does not feel heard or understood. He may consequently learn not to allow himself to feel, or deny the feeling when it next comes up, thinking that it is naughty. The trouble with both of these reactions is that the suppression of the feeling can often lead to depression in the child. The continual non-recognition of feeling can have a serious depressive effect on people of all ages.

The other way of dealing with it is by saying, 'Tommy, what made you so angry that you felt you had to hit Susie?' This way Tommy learns that what he is feeling is called 'angry' and this, along with a few other techniques, will help him manage the feeling the next time because he can acknowledge it.

The first thing a child needs to be taught is that feelings are just feelings. They're neither good, nor bad, they're just feelings. It is the behaviour that the feeling drives that may or may not be acceptable. To believe that the feeling itself is unacceptable is to encourage the child to stop expressing that feeling which, in turn, can lead to unacceptable behaviour. So in this case, Tommy's anger is a perfectly valid emotion — he just needs to learn how to manage it.

2. Name the feeling

The second step is **naming** the feeling. There should be no emotion attached to talking to children about their feelings. Simply teach them to have a large range of feelings and help them realise that these are all acceptable. Teach them that everyone can feel sad, happy, angry, unappreciated, loved, unwanted, excited. They can feel pain, fear, disappointment, frustration and can be just plain scared. Each feeling has a name and the child has to learn to put the right name to the particular feeling.

3. Validate the feeling

The third step is **validating** the feeling. This process is important as it can either build or break self-esteem.

Jasmine comes to her mother and says: 'I can't do my maths homework. I feel really stupid.' What do many parents

Why Won't My Child Listen?

say? Something like 'Don't be silly, of course you're not stupid.' We think we're building a child's self-esteem by telling them that they aren't stupid, when, in fact, what we are doing is invalidating the child's feeling of stupidity as though it doesn't count. If this happens too often, the child will learn to hide their feelings or say nothing — and then we wonder why so many teenagers don't talk to their parents. It's because they are tired of the direct or indirect way in which their parents, despite the best will in the world, tell them they are wrong.

When Jasmine tells her mother she feels stupid, her mum needs to ask her why she feels stupid. In this way she has validated Jasmine's feelings and opened the door for further communication.

4. Express the feeling

The fourth step is **expressing** those feelings. If children realise they will not be laughed at or told they are being silly when they express how they feel, then they will be more inclined to be open about feelings. If they know that their feelings are validated, they feel safe and explore more feelings. After all, our goal as parents is to increase our child's repertoire of feelings.

5. Reframe the feeling

The fifth step is **reframing** negative feelings. Once we accept that the feeling itself is neutral and that it is the interpretation of the trigger event that is driving it, then we can change our feelings by changing our interpretation. The secret here with children is to teach them to identify the trigger or activating event and then check their thinking around that event.

Let's say that Tommy has a favourite toy car and his sister Susie has broken it. Tommy flies into a rage that results in him hitting his sister — as in the first example we gave. We have asked Tommy to acknowledge his feeling by asking him why he is so upset. He says that Susie has broken his car. Why is that such a bad thing?, we ask him. 'It was my favourite toy and now I can't play with it anymore,' he might reply. OK, so let's find a solution. Can another car take its place? This makes him think about the car and what is so special, if anything, about it. That, in turn, may make him think about what is really angering him. Perhaps it is that Susie is just annoying him all the time, not the fact that she broke his car. Help Tommy find the real reason for the anger, then substitute a more helpful, maybe more rational, thought — all without denigrating his original feeling.

6. Manage the feeling

The sixth and last step is **managing** the feeling. This comes about by being able to answer three simple questions:

- Am I hurting anybody else?
- Am I hurting myself?
- Is this achieving what I want to achieve?

If the answer to the first two questions is 'yes', then the feeling needs to be reframed, as it does if the answer to the last question is 'no'.

A positive outcome is that the child reacts appropriately to the feeling, nobody is hurt, and the child has been allowed to achieve whatever it was they wanted from the situation by knowing what they had been feeling, being able to express it without fear of ridicule and having the skill set to change if necessary.

It's a big ask for young children, but you'd be surprised how quickly they adopt this sort of thinking if they are being taught it from an early age.

Here's another example of how you can support your child in learning the value of their feelings. We'll use the feeling of anger as the example. Your two-year-old boy is clearly angry about something.

1. Help him acknowledge that feeling by asking, 'How are you feeling?'
2. Ask him to describe the feeling. Make sure you give the feeling a name — in this case by saying, 'Are you angry?'
3. Validate the feeling by asking him what it feels like to be angry. Then you might ask him what he feels like doing when he is angry. Get him to talk about the feeling — this will help him deal with anger appropriately.

It can be helpful to establish a regular time of day with your child for being quiet and just talking about the day, the good things and the not-so-good things. Get them to open up about their life that day, how they felt about it and what they did and didn't enjoy. Listen to them with respect and validate their feelings at every turn.

"Establish a regular time of day with your child for being quiet and just talking about the day."

Another way to help your child express feelings is through creative output. Get them to draw or paint their feelings — this particularly helps in letting anger go. Set your child up with a pad and crayons and make it a regular part of your day. Get them to do a drawing about their day and encourage them to talk about the drawing. If they are particularly angry with someone, ask them to write a letter to that person setting out exactly how they feel. This can be therapeutic. You don't have to send the letter — just the act of writing it can dissipate the anger appropriately.

Another method is to stimulate the child's senses, particularly through touch, as we discussed in Chapter 11.

13

encouraging children to behave

C hildren are not born knowing how to behave. They are born undisciplined and impulsive, which is why they have parents — to teach them what is expected, to set rules and standards for approved conduct, and to define and enforce consequences for behaviour. Parents can do great harm to children when they neglect to give them this kind of structure.

What exactly constitutes unacceptable behaviour? At this point we will all probably diverge. What is unacceptable to one family may be perfectly OK to another. Behaviour, both acceptable and unacceptable, is largely defined by the values that you hold. In some cases, families believe that anything their child does is acceptable so long as it does not hurt or damage someone else or their property. In other cases, it is unacceptable to behave outside the familial or social norm and children are made to comply with the codes of conduct in place in their environment.

The renowned child psychologist Rudolph Dreikurs said, 'Like a plant needs water, children need encouragement.' He went on to say that they also needed guidance and limits. They depend on their parents to set these limits.[12] Now obviously children up to the age of one are too young to understand boundaries. At this stage in their lives they need love, cuddling and protection.

"Children need guidance and limits."

One- to three-year-olds have very little more sense, but they can understand the word 'no' and that consequences will follow their behaviour. Children of these ages love saying 'no'. They are mimicking their mum or dad and just like hearing the sound of the word. Over-reaction to your child's 'no!' will do nothing more than reinforce their behaviour. The angrier you get, the more they will delight in winding you up. So stop and think for a moment why you are saying 'no'. If what they're doing isn't harmful, unhealthy or life threatening, perhaps you could allow your child to continue and allow whatever it is they are exploring. On the other hand, if their behaviour is, for some reason, unacceptable to you, then tell your child clearly what it is that you want them to do, rather than just saying, 'No, you can't do that.' Very often it is possible to suggest an alternative. For example, if little Anthony is scribbling on the living-room wall, tell him you don't want him writing on the wall, but 'Here is a nice big sheet of paper for you to draw on instead.'

'SHUT UP AND ACT!'

Over the age of three, children begin to understand more and more about cause and effect, and become craftier at trying to get what they want from you.

As the parent it is your job to decide on the boundaries for your child. But there's no point just mouthing platitudes at your children or failing to back up your reprimands with actions. Rudolph Dreikurs formulated this very clear message for parents: 'Shut up and act!' A perfect example of this is what happened when Janet's eldest daughter insisted in borrowing her mother's clothes without asking. Having been asked on several occasions to stop doing it, Janet put a lock on her bedroom door and that was that! You must be prepared to match your words with actions.

"Set the rules and stick to them!"

What Dreikurs actually meant was, set the rules and stick to them. They can be physical rules such as 'The car doesn't start until everyone is in seatbelts', or emotional ones like 'Everyone uses soft voices to each other in this family.' The rules must be simple and clear, and, above all, appropriate to the age of the child in question. But here's the hard part: these rules must apply equally to the adults in the family, too. There's not much point in telling your child, 'We only use soft voices in this house', then Mum and Dad start screaming at each other! Once the rules have been made and explained to the child, the consequences of breaking those rules must also be explained and enforced. When those rules are being broken, further explanations and lectures do not persuade the child to act differently. Trying to be rational with a young child driven by emotion is about as successful as trying to teach a fish to ride a bicycle.

Break time

When a child becomes overemotional and will not listen to reason, you must take action. With children over the age of two, one of the best actions is what we call 'break time'. If your child misbehaves and breaks the rules, then quietly take them to your break-time place. Sit there quietly together for a few minutes without giving them attention of any kind. Don't touch, talk to or even look at them. Then, after a short time, suggest that they try again to do whatever it was that warranted the break time. If you are away from home, you might use your car for your break-time place. The action must immediately follow the behaviour, as children have a short attention span and the effect needs to follow quickly on the heels of the cause. They need a consistent and firm response from you in order to grow up healthy and accountable.

Never argue

Never argue with your child. That is another self-defeating exercise. Always keep your cool and simply restate the rules.

'Oh please, Mummy, can I have just one more chocolate?' begs your daughter.

'You know the rules. Only one chocolate a day,' you reply calmly. She continues to whine, trying to break your resolve.

Validate her dislike of the ruling: 'I know you don't like that rule, but if you eat too many chocolates you will ruin your teeth. The rule stands.'

If she continues to argue or moan about your decision, then it is time to decide which part of the brain she is operating from and use appropriate language to shift her to other parts. (See Chapter 4.)

It is part of your child's development to test your boundaries with whining, crying or even unkind remarks like 'I hate you.' Children are as cunning as little fox cubs — they can figure out exactly how to push your buttons and persuade you to give in. Your job is to withstand the onslaught. This isn't easy, but it is an important lesson that your child has to learn from an early age — 'no' means no. Parents who vacillate and are inconsistent with their rules and boundaries soon lose the respect of their children, which makes it increasingly harder for parents to exercise any control as the children grow up. Reasonable limits and consistent follow-through produce a greater, not a lesser, sense of security and love within your child.

DEALING WITH MISBEHAVIOUR

Misbehaviour is very often an attempt by the child to gain attention. When they cannot gain the level of recognition they want, they will resort to a variety of antisocial behaviours to try to force you into noticing them and acceding to their wishes. The important thing is to stand your ground, stick to the rules and show your child that behaviours such as tantrums, bad language or other antisocial carryings-on will not be tolerated and will result in break time if they don't alter their thinking.

Very often, as harried parents, we are too busy to notice when our children are playing happily. We only tend to notice and react to disruptive or inappropriate behaviour. That, in turn, leads to us reprimanding our children more than praising them. After all, we expect our children to behave well, don't we? It pays, nevertheless, to let them know that!

Try something new

Here's something different that you might like to try. Develop a positive relationship with your child by noticing when they are doing well. For example:

- 'I like the way you played quietly with your doll while Mummy was on the phone.'
- 'I noticed that you picked up all your toys. It helps Dad very much.'

Remarks like these help your child to know what is expected and appreciated. Telling your son he is a 'good boy' or your daughter she is a 'good girl' isn't particularly useful. A fuller explanation is needed to make sense to them. As discussed in Chapter 11, this 'good child' syndrome puts a great deal of stress on children, who believe that they have to be 'good' to please other people, making them fear what will happen to them if they make mistakes which could be construed as 'bad'. The result is that they stop learning what is appropriate behaviour and strive to be 'good'. In doing so they lose touch with their own feelings and conscience, or, to use our animal analogy, only Human Harry is at work and Dolphin Daisy is nowhere to be found.

It is also valuable to explain to your child exactly what is required of them at certain times, and how you want them to behave. For example, you have a friend coming over for afternoon tea and you want some time to talk to her quietly. The conversation with your child prior to her arrival might go like this:

'My friend Judy is coming to talk to me this afternoon. I need to have some quiet, uninterrupted time with her for about 20 minutes, please. After that we will sit down and write out your birthday invitations.'

Having said this, you must make sure you stick to it. If you let the 20 minutes slide into an hour, your child will quite rightly become annoyed and doubt your word.

Then again, you might have this conversation with your young son:

'The Johnstons are coming to tea today and I would like you to share some of your toys with Sam, please. Which toys would you like to share, and which shall we put away in the cupboard?'

Both these examples make it plain to your child exactly what is expected of them. You have spoken to them about a situation in advance and ideally gained their agreement to abide by the rules. You have involved them in the decisions and they feel part of the outcome.

Children tend to behave well when they feel appreciated, listened to and know exactly what is expected of them. That's not to say they won't try it on from time to time, but that's the nature of childhood! Positive behaviour is connected to positive self-esteem. Remember the three building blocks of self-esteem:

- Make your child feel special.
- Make your child feel valued.
- Make your child feel respected.

HOW TO ENCOURAGE DESIRABLE BEHAVIOUR

There are three basic ways in which you can encourage your child to behave well:

1. Describe the kind of behaviour you expect from them.
2. Give clear instructions by telling your child in simple terms what you want them to do.
3. Teach your child to share and play cooperatively.

You might say to your child:

- 'Please ride your bike only on the pavement.'
- 'Hold my hand to cross the road.'
- 'Please sit up at the table.'
- 'Please try to keep your food on your plate.'

You can add to this list to suit yourself. Then, having shown your children the sort of behaviour you expect, it never does any harm to reward them for it. This is called positive reinforcement, which is not to be confused with bribery, and there are numerous ways in which it can be carried out.

The reward chart

Probably the most popular and the most simple form of positive reinforcement is the reward chart. This is used to reward the efforts of the child in trying to change behaviours and act as you would like. It is a good idea to stick with just one behaviour at a time. So, for example, if your child has a tendency to interrupt you when you are speaking, think up a special chart with rewards for them when they don't interrupt you for a specified amount of time. Let them help you choose the sort of chart it is to be. Will it have stickers or smiley faces or stars on it? When is the reward to be given — every evening, every morning? What is the reward? It is a good idea to give small rewards along the way, with a big one at the end when all the squares have been filled in. A powerful reward is special time spent with Mum or Dad, or a special outing just for them. It is not advisable to run a chart on any one particular goal for more than a fortnight — after that it can become tedious for all concerned and lose its effectiveness.

Ignoring inappropriate behaviour

As we have said, inappropriate behaviour is often a child's attempt to gain attention and as such should not be encouraged by the parent either becoming upset about it or, alternatively, spending hours talking about it and explaining why it is wrong. The best approach to inappropriate behaviour is to tell your child clearly what you expect them to do, move them away from the present situation and set them to doing something different.

If you are consistent in this, it won't take long for the child to realise that they won't get far by continuing the behaviour.

> *"The best approach to inappropriate behaviour is to tell your child clearly what you expect them to do."*

Act immediately

To stop a child from carrying on with a particular type of behaviour, you need to act immediately. First, tell the child to *stop* what they are doing, give them five seconds and if the behaviour has not stopped, then implement the consequences. For example: 'Johnny, stop arguing with your sister about the TV or it will be turned off.' Johnny continues, five seconds later you turn the TV off. Asking a child to *do* something might involve a little more leeway — 'Johnny, please pack your toys away.' Wait five seconds, then: 'Johnny, please pack your toys away or I will confiscate your Action Man.' Another five seconds, then take Action Man and lock him in a cupboard and pocket the key.

TO SMACK OR NOT TO SMACK?

No discussion about behaviour, rules and discipline would be complete without mentioning the subject of smacking. We do not agree with inflicting violence of any sort on a child, and certainly never when angry. Hitting children is like hitting animals of any kind: it is counter-productive and instils instinctive resentment in the one being hit, which may have long-lasting detrimental effects. This said, however, there is the odd occasion when a short, sharp smack — only ever to the buttocks — may be necessary. Such an event would involve the child doing something that might have an immediate effect on his or her safety such as lighting a match or running out into the road — a rare event calling for a rare remedy. Ultimately, punishments such as the loss of liberty, access to television or a favourite toy have a far more beneficial effect on a child than a whack on the behind.

14

modifying your child's behaviour

We have looked at ways to encourage children to behave and examined what is acceptable and unacceptable behaviour. Now we will look at some ways in which you can actively play a part in modifying your children's behaviour.

DEFINING THE PROBLEM

So many parents call us up and say, 'My son simply won't listen, he won't do as he is told.'

We ask: 'What is he not listening to? Give examples.'

'He won't go to the bathroom when I want him to have a bath' is a common response. So why won't he go to the bathroom? There are many issues to be considered when we think children are not listening.

Check focus

For a start, what are children physically doing when we talk to them? If they are not brain integrated and not focusing, then they physically do not hear or see you when you tell them what to do. So if your child is playing with their Lego and is intent on what they are doing, first you need to get their focus dimension balanced. This will enable them to have a wider perspective to be able to respond. You can do this by bending down, coming into their vision, then using language they will respond to. Talk about what they are building, then use a colourful piece of Lego to move their eyes out of the narrow range so they can take in more of their space. The time is now right to talk about the bath.

What is your intention?

Intent is another important aspect of the equation. Why do we want the child to have a bath exactly at that moment? Many parents would say the reason is that they have a number of children and need order in their lives. There are two sides to this argument. Children do respond well when their environment is ordered and they know what to expect, and they know what is expected of them. However, rigidity in parents almost always causes rebellion — even at a very young age.

> *"Children respond well when their environment is ordered, they know what to expect, and what is expected of them."*

Potty training is a perfect example of this. Patricia's two-year-old daughter would not go on the toilet when she was asked to. When she refused, Patricia put her back in nappies and for a week or more after that the child did not pass a stool. Patricia was beside herself. We advised Patricia to try to relax, that her daughter would not burst. She replied seriously that she thought she would because she ate so much! When asked why it was so important to Patricia to have her daughter toilet trained, she replied that it was because other children around her were. Asked again why that mattered so much, the answer was finally elicited that she felt a failure because her child was still in nappies when others were not.

The *intent* was not a healthy one. It did not take the uniqueness of the child into account and she was disempowered from reaching toilet training in her own time.

Many parents run their lives and those of their children based on the following few intentions:

- What other people think of the parent
- Feeling a failure if milestones are not met (who set the time for these milestones?)
- Making life easier for the parent
- Fear of the child getting out of control
- Wanting a perfect child
- Wanting the child to become what we want them to become

None of these is remotely healthy, either for parent or child, and is bound to result in ultimate unhappiness all round.

Win/Win

In Chapter 19 we discuss win/win tactics. For now, it is vital to remember that the principle of win/win is that both parties feel satisfied at the end of the communication; they both feel heard and good about themselves. If the parent bullies the child into doing something they are not comfortable doing, the parent will have won while the child will not feel OK about themselves and will feel like they have lost. This entices them to find other strategies to try to win next time. In doing so they lose the art of learning to search for ways in which both parties can retain their self-esteem and respect for each other. Often these other strategies are inappropriate behaviour or rebelling against the parent by not listening.

STRATEGIES FOR EFFECTIVE BEHAVIOUR MODIFICATION

Understand the uniqueness of the child

- What parts of the brain do they prefer operating from?
- How do they prefer to learn?
- What behaviour and language motivates them into action?
- How much time do they need to do things?
- What subtle rewards do they receive when they are doing well?

Always search for win/win behaviour

- Both parties must be comfortable after the communication.
- Appropriate behaviour must take place for both parties.
- Both parties need to feel respected.

Use appropriate language

- Use language that is age appropriate. We might use baby talk for too long, or use language that is beyond a child's understanding. Your language needs to be just a little ahead of the child — so they understand, but also learn a little. Using overly advanced language can overwhelm and make a child feel inadequate.
- When talking to your child, be sure to use language that is positive and respectful, and builds their self-esteem.
- Use colourful language. This does not mean swearing — it means language that makes children use their imagination — their right brain.

RESPECTING NEEDS AND FEELINGS

Last but not least, respect the needs and feelings of your child. The following are some ways in which you can do that.

Allow them to express their thoughts

Often children say bizarre things, and often in return adults make comments like 'Don't be silly', 'That's ridiculous' or 'That doesn't exist.' For example, James had an imaginary friend, Molly, whom he talked to and about for years. How would you deal with a situation like that? Here are two different scenarios.

One family openly spoke about Molly when James did, asked questions about her and made no fuss about her. The other family kept saying Molly did not exist — that James was stupid imagining she did and that he should stop talking about her.

In the first scenario, James would have felt heard, validated and understood. He knew he could say anything he felt and thought, and it would be discussed. In the second, James would have felt silly, hurt and would not risk his feelings in the future. He had two choices: to feel angry because he felt misunderstood or to stop feeling and say nothing. It is better that James feels heard. There's plenty of time as he grows older for the imaginary Molly to go.

Notice what they say and how they say it

Children use different expressions based on what they hear in the home and also what they see in their imagination. Often parents are mortified when a three-year-old comes out with four-letter words and they wonder where they get them from — normally from the parents!

The way children describe things is a great clue to what is going on in their minds. Drawings are another way of observing this. At times children draw odd things and the parent will ask, 'What's that?' 'A caterpillar,' answers the child proudly, at which point the parent may laugh and say, 'Oh, it looks more like a train to me.' The child, proud of the caterpillar, feels deflated and is less likely to show the parent the next artistic effort for fear of being laughed at. Was it worth it? No.

Accept their quirks without ridicule

Mikey refused to wear clothes for two years. His mother would religiously dress him every morning but as soon as she went to the next room he would take all his clothes off. He went everywhere naked, turned brown as a berry and was quite happy. (Mind you, he wasn't happy when this evidence was used at his 21st birthday party!) His mother dressed him with no fuss in the morning, staying neutral, and when he had taken the clothes off she would put them in a bag if they were going out (just in case he changed his mind) or back in the cupboard, thereby saving the washing bills.

Children have funny little quirks that really don't matter and usually don't harm anybody — so let them run their course and the phase will end. Most things are just that, a phase. This may be hard to believe when you are right in the centre of the mayhem, but they always do.

Accept their way of doing things

Often children want to wear horrific clothing combinations, or they don't want to wear a jumper when their parents believe it is cold. Respect their choices. They will invariably put on a jumper if they are cold. We so often assume our children must do things the way we do. It is disrespectful and minimising them as people if we assume our way is better. We have no right to believe that. We say things like 'Why don't you do it this way?' What that tells them is that their way is not good enough. If we really think our way may make things easier for them, we could try using language like 'If I were you, I'd probably try to do it this way. But that's OK, we're all different.' A brief explanation as to why you would do it differently can be added, but without trying to force them to adopt your idea. This gives children the power to retain their dignity and remain open so they can look at the other way without feeling put down.

A good example of this was when Myra moved her children from Sydney to Paris for a while. She started buying winter clothes for the children as they were moving in April and she knew that it would still be cold following the European winter. Her eldest son refused to try on long trousers, saying he would always wear his board shorts. He maintained he would never be seen dead in long trousers. Myra didn't make a fuss, but nevertheless bought a few pairs hoping they would fit. He only lasted a few hours in Paris before going in search of his longs! Myra, though dying to say 'I told you so!', sensibly bit her tongue based on the above principles. The boy's dignity remained intact even though her patience was sorely tested.

Silly things can be turning points

Often when we work with adults who have low self-esteem they can trace it back to one incident that triggered their feelings of inadequacy. We often say silly things in jest, make jokes at other people's expense and then say that we are only joking. The subconscious mind of the average child has trouble distinguishing between a joke and the truth, so generally they take on board what is heard. For that reason it is a good idea to think carefully before we say things to children. You can never be sure that they aren't going to take it to heart.

15

setting the
boundaries

A boundary is like a fence bordering a property that defines where one person ends and someone else begins. All children need boundaries and limits to make sense of their world and to help them learn how to regulate their behaviour, and it is up to the parent to modify the child's behaviour with the introduction of appropriate limits to that behaviour.

If we know people's boundaries, we can trust that they will demonstrate self-control. We can expect them to take responsibility for their feelings, behaviours and attitudes.

"Young children want boundaries, even if they don't know it."

Young children want boundaries, even if they don't know it. Boundaries give them a sense of discipline from which they derive security in knowing the limits. It's worth remembering that boundaries can always be expanded, but it's far harder to rein a child in if the boundary has not been established in the first place.

This is one reason why parenting is so tricky. Children are not born with boundaries, so in order for them to learn their roles and responsibilities, parents have to set clear boundaries of their own and help their children do likewise — which is all a lot easier said than done.

These symbolic fences serve three main purposes:

1. To keep people from invading our personal space and abusing us
2. To keep us from going into other people's space and abusing them
3. To give us a sense of who we are and our uniqueness

Both parents and teachers often become quite tense and impatient when children have difficulty learning to self-regulate their behaviour. However, if a child is having difficulty remembering that the word 'apple' starts with an A, or finds that cutting out an accurate circle is a challenge, we tend to be somewhat more relaxed.

Social skills are no different from cognitive, gross motor or fine motor skills. Like all skills, they have to be learned and one of the first lessons worth teaching children is that with clear boundaries they will respond appropriately to situations. Unclear boundaries frequently lead to inappropriate behaviour which can, in turn, lead the child into all sorts of trouble.

And where do children learn these boundaries? Well, like almost everything else, they learn from their parents. If a child's parents do not have healthy personal boundaries, then it is probable that they will learn the same behaviours.

HEALTHY BOUNDARIES

What can generally be considered to be healthy boundaries? Well, these boundaries can be physical, mental and emotional. Examples of physical boundaries include our sense of personal space and privacy. Other physical boundaries may involve clothes, shelter, safety, money, space, noise or smoke pollution and time. Mental and emotional boundaries include our beliefs, feelings, choices, interests, relationships, responsibilities and respect.

In establishing boundaries for your children, it is important to remember where you stand in all this. You need to take time to understand what is going on with your child and coach them through this learning process. If a child misbehaves, then the first step is to find out the motive behind the misbehaviour. You can do this by asking: 'Why do you do that? I want to understand. Are you angry or hurt about something?'

Often children will misbehave in reaction to something causing them stress or pain. Find out what is causing the behaviour and the cure becomes much easier. Being bullied at school, for example, is a fairly typical cause of misbehaviour at home. If you adopt the 'I want to understand the reasons for your behaviour' approach and are patient with the child, rather than being overbearing and insistent on an immediate answer, then you are likely to discover that the child is the victim of bullying. Once that is acknowledged, you can take steps to prevent it and in doing so the child's behaviour will generally quickly improve.

Just like any enterprise involving a group of people, there have to be some rules for a household to run smoothly. In the case of children, rules need to be clear and simple, and, of course, age appropriate. When placing limits on a child, remember that as soon as the child has proved they can operate well within these limits, then the boundary fence can be extended a bit more and a bit more.

There are many parents we know who don't like the idea of imposing too many rules on their children. This approach, however, generally ends up with the parents creating a rod for their own backs. If you don't lay down a set of rules at an early age, children are likely to grow up not paying much attention to other people's feelings and are likely to be manipulative, non-responsive to the needs of others and lacking in trust.

Parents with healthy personal boundaries know when it is appropriate to say 'yes' and 'no'; they respect and look after themselves, tend not to blame others for their failings, take responsibility for their feelings and actions, respect other people and won't let others abuse them. When this is translated into the family, it usually means that children feel confident to talk about their feelings without the threat of being criticised or laughed at, they feel respected, that their differences and uniqueness are valued, they are honest, their privacy is respected, they feel safe and the consequences of inappropriate behaviour are clear and consistently applied.

Teaching cause and effect

This basic rule deals with consequences — if you do that, this will happen. Many parents misapply the rule by using punitive consequences, such as becoming angry, smacking the child, nagging and withdrawing their love. Instead, they would be better off using practical consequences, such as losses of time, money, possessions or promised outings, which in the long run will prove far more beneficial. These kinds of consequences yield long-term results, whereas punitive consequences generally don't. This can be confirmed by the fact that children who are given the choice of a smacking or having their pocket money docked, frequently choose the smacking because it is over and done with quickly and soon forgotten. That is another good reason why smacking a child is seen as physical abuse with no valuable long-term goal.

As we discussed in Chapter 13, the consequence of an action should be appropriate to it. Assuming that you have paused and thought whether the child's action warrants a consequence or not, make that consequence a natural outcome of the behaviour. For example, if a child continually refuses to help tidy up toys, then cancel a planned outing they were looking forward to as a result. If your son doesn't do his homework, he misses out on watching TV with the rest of the family. If your daughter is rude to you, then next time she has her favourite toy confiscated for 48 hours.

It is best to save this rule for serious incidents and the consequences should follow the offence as quickly as possible.

The younger the child, the more immediate should be the consequences. With very young children, a firm 'no' and isolation or removal from the situation will generally do the trick.

THE TWO MAJOR BOUNDARIES

There are two main types of boundaries which we, as parents, need to set our children. One is external, the other is internal.

External boundaries

External boundaries involve physical and sexual limits and it is important that children understand these from an early age. Physical limits relate principally to how close people can come to each other. In Australia, we are used to a lot of open space and most Australians don't feel comfortable when people come too close physically, whereas in Europe and Asia people are more used to being close to each other. Coming too close to someone without their permission is seen as a violation of their personal space. The best way to check your limits, and those of your children, is to ask someone to walk towards you, looking you in the eye. Note the distance at which you begin to feel that your space is being invaded.

Sexual limits are a challenge for all parents. We need to teach children from an early age to respect their bodies and to understand — by talking with them openly about the body and its various functions without scaring them — that it is not right for people to touch them in certain places. A touch by a relative or a friend, which can be perfectly innocent, can be disturbing for a child. Often adults will kiss and hug children despite them not wanting to be touched at that moment. When someone wants to hug our child against their wishes, we might say, 'Don't be silly, you know John — let him give you a kiss.' In this way we give children the message that they have no right to develop physical boundaries, which, in turn, increases a child's vulnerability to sexual abuse: we have given them the message that adults can do what they want and the child's wishes are not relevant. If a child does not want to be hugged or kissed at a certain moment, their space must be respected and parents should support this.

Sexual abuse is more prevalent than most of us realise. Children who live in an environment where they have no direct or complete information about their body or their sexual development, and are rarely allowed to develop their physical boundaries, quickly lose confidence and are more likely to become the victims of abuse.

We need to encourage children to know what they are feeling — we can do this by talking about feelings then discussing how these feelings translate in their bodies. By using stories and puppets, talking about scary, exciting, happy or funny things, we can help children to vocalise how they feel. For example, how their heart beats faster during a scary film, or their hands grow sweaty on a frightening ride. Then, if they find themselves in an uncomfortable or scary situation, they can feel these warning signs in their body.

Children also need to know that they have a trustworthy network system of adults whom they can go to for help, both inside and outside the family. These are adults with whom the child feels comfortable and to whom they can talk freely about how they feel and, in particular, if they feel that another adult has transgressed healthy boundaries.

We need to teach children to be able to say: 'Stop that! I don't like it.' You can help them to practise this within the family — for example, when they are being tickled. Some children love being tickled, others don't. Teach your child to say 'Stop it!' if they aren't enjoying it, and then stop what you are doing immediately. Perhaps your child is with a friend who starts to play a little too roughly. Teach your child to know that they can ask the friend to stop and be on hand where possible to ensure that the other child respects these wishes.

"We need to teach children to be able to say: 'Stop that! I don't like it.'"

Inevitably some children will face various forms of bullying in their lives. Bullies often pick on children who:

- Look or feel different
- Are stressed at home or at school
- Have a disability
- Struggle with schoolwork
- Are not good at sport
- Lack social confidence

Children are not always prepared to come forward and admit that they are being bullied, and cannot always cope with the problem by themselves. There are various tell-tale signs that parents can look for, however:

- Newly acquired aggressive behaviour
- Withdrawn behaviour
- Thumb sucking
- Bed wetting
- Nail biting
- Nightmares
- Difficulty with sleeping
- Not wanting to go to school
- Finding excuses for avoiding attendance at school
- Wanting to walk or go to school a different way
- Avoiding friends or saying that they have no friends
- Unexplained scratches and bruises
- Responding to questions about unexplained injuries with vague answers

If your child exhibits any of these signs, they may not necessarily have a problem with bullying, but you do need to look into what is worrying your child.

Internal boundaries

Internal boundaries relate to our thinking, feeling and behaviour. If we feel we are not worthwhile, we will allow other people to dominate us. We will not respect the fact that

DEALING WITH BULLYING

Here are a few pointers that parents can use to deal with bullying:

- Find out about the school's bullying policy at enrolment time and ask how this policy manifests itself in the school.

- Discuss with your child what bullying means, why it occurs and what to do if it does occur.

- As much as possible, help children work out their own ways of dealing with the problems.

- Encourage a special time at home after school to talk about the day.

- Listen to your child and take their fears and concerns seriously.

- Avoid calling your child names, such as 'sook' or 'wimp', and don't let anyone else do so, either.

- Let children know that bullying is wrong.

- A child who is confident and self-assured is far less likely to be bullied.

we have a right to our own opinions and feel confident enough to state these clearly. This lack of self-worth is the result of parents who have constantly told us we are wrong. We have therefore stopped trusting what we feel. This will, in turn, affect our behaviour and we are more likely to become subservient, doing things to please other people although we don't really want to do them. Children who have low self-esteem are likely to have unhealthy internal boundaries, which can manifest themselves in the form of 'walls', where the child will go into a shell for fear of being hurt or criticised. There children will not trust anyone and will refuse to display what they are feeling.

As we discussed in Chapter 10, often our internal boundaries are the result of the way we have been spoken to and treated by our parents and other members of our family. It is important to realise that the things we say to our children — even the seemingly harmless throwaway lines — can have a disastrous effect on the more sensitive of our offspring.

Good internal boundaries are created through creating a sense of self-worth in your child. Let them know that they have a right to their opinion, however daft you might think it is, and that they have a right to express it openly and without fear of being ridiculed.

16

the importance
of play

If there's one thing that children enjoy more than practically anything else in the world, it's playing. Most children are naturally playful and it is predominantly through play that they learn about life at the preschool stage. The importance of play in the raising of children cannot be overstated, so, as adults, it is helpful if we can contact our inner child and spend lots of time playing with our children.

Unfortunately, the value of playing is grossly underrated in today's adult society. Before you embark on any kind of leisure activities with your children, it is worth stopping for a moment to think about the why, how and when of adult-organised activities.

PLAY IS NOT TRIVIAL

According to Dr Thomas Armstrong, an American educationalist, many parents regard free play as rather trivial in the lives of their children and would much rather see their kids involved in formal games, educational classes and organised sports. However, he says, research suggests that free play may actually be healthier for your children than these more structured activities. According to Armstrong, pretend play allows children to test their ideas about the world and modify them as they go along. It also helps them to work out emotional conflicts in creative ways and offers a miniature world within which they can learn about social interactions and interpersonal relationships.

> *Parents need to give their kids plenty of room to play. That means being willing to put up with some loudness and horseplay, as long as it doesn't become destructive. It also means providing a few resources, such as old clothes for dress-up activities, blocks or other building materials, outdoor play equipment, and an indoor playhouse or similar enclosure for fantasy play. Giving your child a chance to unleash his or her creative imagination provides them with some basic building blocks, important for success in later life.*[13]

There are many other lessons that children learn simply from playing with each other. Rough-and-tumble play among boys, for example, is an early lesson in leadership. American researcher Tom Reed reported on a group of children between six and nine years of age who regularly played rough-and-tumble games together. He noticed that the younger boys took their lead from the older ones when it came to the rules of the game, since none of these was actually written down. The younger boys accepted that the older ones knew the rules and deferred to them. If the oldest boy took it upon himself to change the rules, when asked why, he would reply, 'Because I'm the oldest and can make the rules.' If an even older boy joined the group, then everyone immediately deferred to him. Since rough-and-tumble games usually start in infancy between father and son, Reed believes that this is the foundation of the recognition of older males as leaders.

"There are many other lessons that children learn simply from playing with each other."

HOW PLAY DEVELOPS INTELLIGENCE

The early-20th-century Swiss scientist Jean Piaget came to the conclusion that intelligence is developed by children's interaction with their peers, teachers and the environment. He believed that all children go through the same developmental stages and that they progress through each stage in a fixed sequence. As children progress through these developmental stages, the exploration behaviours of infants are transformed into the logical intelligence of adolescence and adulthood. One crucial part of this sequence, according to Piaget, was make-believe play. This gives children the opportunity to participate in cultural activities by acting out familiar scenes they observe in daily life, such as playing at doctors and nurses. This type of play provides the child with important insights into the links between the self and the wider community.

USING PLAY FOR LEARNING

From the parents' point of view, perhaps the most important and valuable aspect of playing with your child is that you are

PLAY IN YOUR EVERYDAY ROUTINE

Incorporate playfulness into your everyday routine activities. How can you do this? Well, here's an example.

Four-year-old Alex doesn't love bath-time — his parents can never get him into the bath without a great deal of kicking and screaming. Like most small boys, he has an aversion to soap and water! Alex doesn't like the bath because it means interrupting his playtime, and it is true, he's hated soap ever since some of it got in his eyes and they stung a lot.

To encourage him into the bath, first see if you can negotiate with him about the time of the bath, perhaps leaving a little time for playing after it is done. If he really has an aversion to the soap, then think of alternative products — such as bubble bath — to take its place, and then *make it fun*!

'OK, Alex. Bet you can't beat me crawling to the bathroom!'

or

'Let's pretend we're kangaroos and hop into the bathroom!'

or . . . well, you've got the picture. You can think up an endless variety of similar activities. The point is that few children can resist an invitation to play games, so work them into the routine.

spending positive, quality time with them, being attentive and making them feel valued and important. This time isn't necessarily for teaching them anything, it's just enjoying each other's company and helping them to feel wanted.

Remember Mia, the five-year-old from Chapter 7? Her father was complaining to us that she wouldn't play with him. They were playing 'schools' and Dad was trying to make Mia get her sums right! That wasn't what Mia wanted at all. She wanted to play. She wanted to be the teacher and have the chance of bossing Dad about, but he definitely wasn't getting the point. What she wanted was a 'game' and because she didn't see what they were doing as a game, she was refusing to play.

This is a common scenario. Parents often try to use play to facilitate learning: they 'play' at schools to teach children to spell, they 'play' monopoly to teach them to add. As far as children are concerned, this isn't play. The lightness has been taken out of the process and teaching has taken over as the primary reason. Of course there is a place for 'learning', but it needs to be clearly differentiated from 'playing'.

Children learn a lot from playing as all their senses are engaged. They are listening, looking, touching and even, at times, imagining that they are tasting and smelling. This is a wonderful opportunity to get to know your child. You begin to see what's going on inside — they reveal some of their inner self and you can often determine what they like, what they would like and exactly where their dreams lie. Play is a wonderful avenue for building self-esteem and presents an opportunity for parents to validate the children's imagination and join in their dreams, which gives them the message that they are OK and they are loved.

This is a time when parents run the risk of denting their child's self-esteem if they're not careful. We don't want to be alarmist about this, but refusing to 'play' with your child can have the opposite effect on them. Like Mia, whose Dad wanted to manipulate the game to teach her maths, children know play from work. They receive subliminal messages that they are not worth the time just to be with, and that every minute must be taken up with an ulterior motive.

The dangers of criticism

There is an even more destructive parental trait which should be avoided at all costs, and that is criticising a child at play, trying to give advice or suggesting better ways of doing things. This may seem innocuous, but it slowly erodes a child's self-confidence until they become unsure of themselves and start either trying to please others or becoming difficult as they try desperately to prove to others and themselves that they are worthwhile.

"Even in play, positive language, validating and complimenting and congratulating the child is vital for their wellbeing."

TIME FOR LEISURE

What is leisure? Some people think it means doing nothing. Others look upon leisure as a time for fishing or playing golf or sitting in the garden with their feet up reading a good book. Leisure means different things to different people, but one definition that generally applies to everyone is that it is a time free from work or duty. It is important that we distinguish between leisure (free time) and activities. Free time, as the words suggest, is the time when we are free to do things we enjoy and are not committed to doing if we choose not to. It implies spontaneity. Activities, on the other hand, are more structured and usually need a commitment to attend frequently or regularly, or may require practice. These include things such as learning to play a musical instrument or taking the children to organised sport or ballet.

Why is leisure so important?

It is easy to become caught up in a round of activities that eat up real free time. There is so much out there today from which you can choose. Everyone sets themselves up as experts, and parents often become confused with how many activities to select and how regularly their child should attend. The outcome of this can leave the family with very little unstructured leisure time. Everyone needs time to 'veg out'. It is important that we do not set children up to believe that every minute of their waking day should be planned and filled with adult-driven, organised activities.

As a rule of thumb, here is a guide to the number of extracurricular activities a child should ideally undertake depending on age:

0–5 years   None are necessary (just being able to play is all they need)
5–7 years   One per week
7–12 years   Two per week
12–17 years   As many as you can possibly fit in to keep them busy without neglecting schoolwork!

The need to be slow

Children are not born obsessed with speed. Yet somehow very quickly they have their entire days filled with activities, something for which we parents largely have to take the blame. Naturally we all want the best for our children, but a lot of people think that means exposing them to a wide variety of different stimuli at an early age. Maybe it's the Suzuki Method for budding five-year-old violinists, or computer camps for the tiny Bill Gateses of this world. Anything, just as long as they are doing something, rather than just idling the time away 'playing'.

There is a growing school of thought among education-alists and paediatricians that forcing young children to fill up every minute of their days with sporting and educational activities can be both physically and psychologically harmful. One of the leading proponents of allowing children to slow down is Kathy Hirsh-Pasek, professor of Child Psychology at

Temple University in Philadelphia. According to Professor Hirsh-Pasek, the modern concept of making every minute count is wrong. She did tests on 120 American preschool children, 60 of whom went to nursery schools which emphasised social interaction and play, and 60 who went to schools where academic achievement, even at that early age, was paramount.

'When you look at the scientific evidence,' she says, 'it is clear that children learn better and develop more rounded personalities when they learn in a more relaxed, less regimented, less hurried way.'[14] Alarmed by the current trend toward creating baby Einsteins, Hirsh-Pasek urges parents to step back and practise the three Rs: Reflect, Resist and Recentre. Instead of pushing preschoolers into academically oriented programs that focus on early achievement, she suggests that children learn best through simple playtime, which enhances problem-solving skills, attention span, social development and creativity. 'Play is to early childhood as gas is to a car,' she says, going on to explain that reciting and memorising will only produce 'trained seals' rather than creative thinkers.

"Children learn best through simple playtime, which enhances problem-solving skills, attention span, social development and creativity."

This is an important principle which parents might be well advised to follow right through their child's upbringing, for the pressures can become greater and the effects more harmful the older the child becomes.

CHOOSING SUITABLE ACTIVITIES

There are three particularly important factors in choosing suitable activities for your child, and they all relate to you, the parent. It is easy to quickly find yourself overcommitted financially, emotionally and physically if you are not careful. How many parents do you know who complain that they are running a non-stop taxi service for their children? Jimmy's off to football, Kylie's doing ballet, Sofia has swimming training — and all within half an hour of each other in three different locations!

A young mum recently described to us a family she knew. 'There are four or five children who are constantly being ferried in countless different directions to countless different activities,' she related. 'The family is never at home, and when they are, it is out with the mower, mow the lawn and then into the car and off again to the next round of activities. There is no time for the children to be together as a family, no time to veg out.' We suspect she was talking about her own life!

To avoid this, it is worth taking a long look at your existing commitments and deciding how much time and energy is warranted or available for all these pursuits. For starters, children under five don't need extra activities. In reality they need very little extra planned for them until they become teenagers. If we fill primary school children's days to overflowing, by the time they reach their teen years they will often rebel and refuse to participate. They will be all burnt out activity-wise.

Remember that children don't have the same level of commonsense that you have. Often they will beg you to be allowed to take on another activity — it might be horse-riding lessons or piano playing or swimming lessons — because their best friends are doing it. Before agreeing, carefully consider your response. Is it going to be an added burden for you? Is it, in reality, going to mean that your child is taking on too much? Maybe you can solve it by saying something like: 'Certainly you can learn ballet next term. Which other activity do you want to give up in its place?'

In this way you are signalling to your child that the family resources, both financial and physical, will not stretch to unlimited activities. Explain to the child that it is important for the family to have some time at home just relaxing together. You might also like to explain that the family budget will only allow a couple of activities per child. After all, it is perfectly all right to say 'no' to your child.

Which activities?

Here are some tips to help you decide which activity will be best for your child.

- Take time to research the activity. It is vital that you make a list of criteria and listen to objective, professional advice. What is right for your neighbour, sister or friend may not necessarily be right for you and your children.

- Don't worry about having to make the 'right' decision? Activities don't have to be right — they are merely part of life — some will add something to the child's life, others will not and it does not really matter, they are merely experiences.
- Measure your results against your criteria, weigh the information and trust your own gut feeling.
- While it is valuable to involve your child in the decision-making process initially, it is important not to give the final decision to very young children. We have had parents come to us at a preschool and say, 'I will bring him along and see if he wants to come here.' This is not a decision that a four-year-old can make! Of course, as children grow older and become more mature they can be trusted to make decisions for themselves, but remember, in the end it is you who has to pay the bill!

If possible try to choose activities in which the child has already expressed an interest, but be prepared to accept the fact that you may not always have chosen wisely. Listen to what your child has to say. If they want to leave an activity and you feel that their concerns are unjustified, try to encourage them to stay in the activity at least until the end of term. Meanwhile, investigate their concerns. They may well be right — there may be something about that particular activity that isn't working out.

There is nothing wrong in exposing your child to many different activities over the years, but remember that it is meant to be leisure, and leisure is meant to be fun! If you find that your child's skills are not improving, that they are no longer having fun and are not prepared to put in the practice that is required, then it may well be time to try something new.

Some parents force their children to learn a musical instrument, often the piano, for years, because they did (or didn't and wish they had!). This can be purgatory for a child who isn't musically inclined. If the child enjoys music, the chances are they will enjoy music lessons and will be willing to practise. If not, forget it! No amount of cajoling or force is going to turn Peter into Paganini or Simone into Schubert. Move on to something else, after discussing it with your child.

So what activity do you choose and how? After all, there are so many to choose from. Enlist the help of other members of the family and friends who know your child a year before you would like your child to start some activities. Preschool and playgroups are both good venues for generating ideas and your child's preschool teacher will probably be able to give you good, unbiased advice on what your child would like to do.

Swimming is a popular one to start with and there are a range of inexpensive swimming options run by the Department of Sport and Recreation, generally through the summer school holidays. Also, if you are lucky enough to live in an area that has a swim centre, they generally run classes suited to all ages.

AVOIDING THE SHOPPING BLUES

Shopping with young children can be an absolute nightmare, as every parent knows. Let's face it, we adults don't find it that much fun, so why should children? But it doesn't have to be boring for them. There's one golden rule before you start: *never* take a tired child on a shopping expedition — unless you want to encourage tantrums in the supermarket. How often do you see mums in supermarkets straight after school, when the child is tired and wants to get home and relax and play?

If, however, the time is appropriate and the child is old enough, you can make it fun for them by giving them their own trolley or little basket and a list of items for them to collect. Shopping can then be turned into a mini treasure hunt. When you broach the idea of going shopping and encounter resistance from your child, tell them that if they help you in your shop(s), then they can visit a shop of their choice afterwards. Give and take is in itself a valuable lesson to learn.

Assess your needs

Now's a good time to take stock of your values and reflect on what is important to you. Consider the following: why have you made the choice you have? Why is it important? The choice is important because ultimately it will determine your child's future, friendships and contentment. If your child is unhappy, this will be detrimental to the entire family.

So to help you in your choice, here's a list of factors to consider when assessing your needs, the needs of your child, whatever age they may be, and those of your family, and choosing a suitable activity. Cross out the ones that don't apply and see what you're left with. Then make your decision.

- My child needs a warm, caring, nurturing environment.
- My child needs a stimulating, challenging environment with caring emphasis.
- My child needs action-based activity.
- My child thrives with competition.
- My child is a loner and would benefit from a team-based activity.
- My child dislikes sport.
- We have limited time on weekends.
- We have unlimited time on weekends.
- I would like my child to develop skills to be used in later life.
- I would like my child to establish friendships.
- I would like my child to be part of a team.
- I would like my child to have fun.
- I would like my child to contribute to the community.
- I would like my child to develop independent skills.
- I would like my child to be outdoors.
- I would like my child to have more physical activity.

We recently heard a heart-wrenching story of a mother who withdrew her child from the netball team because she was not allowed to play in the under-tens with her friends. The coach wanted only the best children in the team so that they could win at school matches. This parent believed that sport should be about fun for young children this age and made her feelings known, but to no avail, so she removed her child from the sport.

Similarly, we witnessed a young mother not long ago walking along the path to soccer at 8 o'clock in the morning. Trailing along behind her was a reluctant four-year-old boy, dressed in all the soccer regalia, head down, feet dragging, whose body language clearly indicated he was not happy and excited to be attending competitive soccer. So why was he going? Listen to your children, watch other children and heed what they are telling us . . . 'We are children only once in a lifetime,' they are crying. 'Let us be free to play.'

Let's finish with a checklist you might like to consider when next thinking about an activity for one of your children:

- Has my child shown any interest in this activity?
- Have I realistically costed all the alternatives? Does the activity fit comfortably into the family budget?
- Does my child have the skills and stamina to participate?
- Does the activity reflect my values and those of my partner, and the values we try to promote within the home?
- Do the people in charge respect the children in their care?

- Are parents welcome?
- Is it a non-competitive environment and is no pressure put on the children to perform? (This is an area where self-esteem can be damaged, if the child is not naturally inclined to be sporty and is forced to be competitive. Some children will be naturally competitive, while others may never be.)
- Is everyone given a fair go and an equal chance to participate?
- Are there not too many rules?
- And above all, is it *fun*?

And you might add, does it involve one hour or less of your time per week? If you can say 'yes' to all the above, then go for it and your child should be as happy as a pig in mud!

17

healthy eating

I t is a sad fact that more children in Western countries are becoming obese. This is mainly due to the huge growth over recent decades in consumption of junk foods and the rise of the fast food market. In 1995 the *American Journal of Preventive Medicine* flagged the modern American diet as public health enemy number one, and in more recent years reports in Britain and Australia have confirmed this. Poor nutritional choices cause every bit as much cancer, death, disability and chronic disease as do cigarettes and other drugs.

The Australian prevalence of obesity and overweight is high. According to the 1995 National Nutrition Survey some 45 per cent of men and 29 per cent of women are overweight, of which 18 per cent of men and women are classified as obese. What is more, the prevalence of overweight and obesity in Australia, as in much of the world, appears to be increasing. There is evidence that the proportion of the adult population who are overweight and obese has increased dramatically over the past 15 years, and that obesity appears to be increasing among Australian children and adolescents.

In addition, the costs associated with obesity both in social terms and the implications for a nation's health bill, are staggering. In Australia, the national cost of obesity in 1997 was $464 million, excluding the costs of treating heart disease, a large portion of which is also related to obesity. At the same time in New Zealand the cost is estimated at $303 million. Indirect costs associated with worker absenteeism and premature death in Australia are estimated to account for an additional $272 million. These costs are high, not only in terms of premature death and health care, but also in terms of disability and a diminished quality of life

WHY CHILDREN BECOME OBESE

There is only one place where these alarming figures can be counteracted and that is in the home. Children become obese for four basic reasons: they are being served the wrong type of foods; they lack exercise; they are unhappy; or they are bored with the food they are offered. Parents play an important role in establishing healthy eating habits in young children. By buying, preparing and offering healthy food to children, you are setting them up for optimal functioning and happiness in all areas of their life. This needs to start from an early age. A wide variety of healthy foods will quickly make the child familiar with a diet that is both varied and good for their health.

Instilling healthy eating habits in children is far easier said than done, however. Parents can help here by being good role models and eating healthy food themselves. How can you expect your child to respect a healthy diet if they see Mum or Dad scoffing on a hamburger and chips or a greasy hotdog?

Dr Alan Greene, an American paediatrician, tells a lovely story about his small son and the power of imitation. 'I can remember the brave little face of my son,' he recounts. 'I was drinking a cup of coffee. My boy kept asking for a sip. I declined by saying that it tastes yucky to kids and making a face. He persisted, and I gave him a little sip. His face combined shock, disgust and disappointment. His eyes got big and watered. Then he smiled and said, "More." It reminded me of the time I smoked a cigar offered to me by an older boy on a scouting trip. Kids' desire to imitate at this stage is a deep, powerful force. Tap into it.'[15]

Over the years most of us have accumulated a whole portfolio of unhealthy habits. Having a child is the perfect opportunity to break them and start anew. When your children want to imitate you, the parent, make sure that what they are imitating is healthy.

To quote Dr Greene again: 'When you give children good nutrition, you are giving them the nutrient-building blocks that literally become the eyes you look into; the knees that get scraped; the bones that support their growing bodies; their inquisitive, curious brains; and the hearts that pump quietly night and day down through the years.'

We couldn't have put it better ourselves!

DON'T FIGHT OVER FOOD

What do you do if your children dislike the food you are feeding them, even though it is nourishing and healthy? Well, first of all, don't have a fight about it. Fighting with children over food is as pointless as trying to force a pork chop down the throat of a vegan. If the child is old enough, ask them what they like to eat before you prepare the meal and, assuming it is on the healthy list, serve them that. If the child isn't quite at an age when they can explain what they want, then try a wide variety of different foods and make a note of the ones that slip down without a fuss, and remember to avoid the foods that land up on the floor. Here's a true story which illustrates the point perfectly.

Katie, an eight-months-pregnant mum with two-year-old toddler Charlie in tow, went to the supermarket at the end of an exhausting day to buy a quick six items. It would only take a few minutes and Charlie behaved beautifully, sitting happily in the trolley at the checkout. All of a sudden he decided to jump down off the trolley and dash like greased lightning, as only a two-year-old can, to a distant corner of the supermarket. Poor Kate was forced to leave her groceries unpaid for at the checkout while she mustered as much speed as an eight-months-pregnant woman can to chase after him. She finally retrieved Charlie, returned to the checkout, paid her bill and headed home. A little time later, she sat Charlie down to a dinner of meat, cheese, lettuce and carrot. 'I want Weeties,' demanded Charlie. Kate patiently explained that they don't eat Weeties for dinner, and that Charlie had had Weeties already for breakfast. Being a typical two-year-old, Charlie persisted: 'I want Weeties! I want Weeties! I want Weeties!' At the end of her tether, Kate took a handful of Weeties and threw them over the top of Charlie's salad, saying, 'Here are your Weeties!' At which point Charlie happily ate all his dinner, Weeties and salad all mixed in together.

The moral of that story is simple: don't turn mealtimes into a battlefield. It just isn't worth it, and as long as your child is happy with the food and eats it, don't worry about how disgusting the mixture may be!

"Fighting with children over food is as pointless as trying to force a pork chop down the throat of a vegan."

It is also a stressful and unnecessary exercise to try to force a child to eat when they are not hungry. There is a school of thought that says it is OK for children to snack throughout the day, rather than sit down to regular meals. We don't really agree with that philosophy, although the occasional healthy snack, carrot sticks and the like, are all right between meals. It is preferable, for a range of reasons, to make the child sit at a table for meals. It improves digestion, enhances family togetherness and helps the child to understand that there are certain times of the day for doing different activities. So, ask the child to sit at the table with you, but don't force them to eat unless they want to. Explain, however, that there is no more food on offer until the next scheduled meal. They'll eat plenty when they're hungry and, believe us, there's no danger of them starving!

THE FIVE RULES OF HEALTHY EATING

The details of what is and what is not a balanced diet are well documented, so we won't go into them here. We are more concerned with the effects that particular foods have on the behaviour of your child. So let's just recap the five simple rules of healthy eating to set you on the right course:

1. Set an example by always eating a variety of healthy food.
2. Prepare meals that are pleasing to a child's eye — for example, present foods of different colours and textures.
3. Start introducing new tastes, especially green vegetables, from very early on. Six months is not too early to start.
4. Never force a child to eat. Mealtime should never be a time for fighting.
5. Avoid high-sugar snacks in between meals. Ideally try to avoid the child snacking altogether so that they are sufficiently hungry by mealtimes.

Of course, everybody enjoys a 'treat' now and again — that sinful chocolate bar or a nice fattening bag of oil-drenched chips — but try to keep these for special occasions rather than making them an everyday event.

THE EFFECT OF FOOD ON BEHAVIOUR

It has been intensively researched and accepted by many experts that food and food additives have an impact on the behaviour of some children. Each child arrives in the world with their own unique genetic pattern and over a period of time the build-up of sugar, chemicals and other pollutants in the small body of the child can cause an adverse reaction which often manifests as inappropriate behaviour.

SOME SHOCKING STATISTICS

Fascinating new research done recently in Wales at Cardiff University's Regeneration Institute came up with the following alarming findings:

- Shocking Statistic No. 1: One in five children in Britain is overweight and one in 10 is classed as obese.

- Shocking Statistic No. 2: Eight per cent of children have nothing to eat at home before school, and almost all of the A$1031 million spent annually on food and drink on the way to and from school goes on confectionery, chips and canned drinks.

All of this, according to the report, has a seriously adverse effect on children's learning ability and academic performance.[16]

All the evidence points to exactly the same sort of situation beginning to take place here in Australia.

The role that these play in cases of ADD and ADHD remains controversial, but there seems to be no doubt that some foods can aggravate the condition in a number of children. Studies have shown that up to 60 per cent of children with ADHD have increased behavioural problems such as overactivity, aggression and violence after consuming sugar, preservatives and food colourings.

Many parents have reported moodiness, temper tantrums, hyperactivity and aggressiveness following a large intake of sugar by their child. We know of a case where a small girl who was allowed a commercially produced cheese-flavoured snack product as a treat every Friday night always became very bad-tempered the following day, until a naturopath diagnosed a sensitivity to one or more of the additives in the product. A change to another brand of snack food without additives cured the problem immediately.

The best way to prevent possible intolerances is to feed children fresh fruit and vegetables (organic where possible) as the major part of each meal. Children prefer cut-up fruit and vegetables to whole — make it easy for them to eat!

Different children react differently to different things, but if your child appears listless, often tired without due reason, has reoccurring colds or ear and throat infections, dark circles under the eyes, asthma or eczema, they may be suffering from some food intolerance or allergy. In such a case, seek advice from your health professional — either a doctor or a naturopath.

If your child exhibits an intolerance to any food, then it is bound to have an adverse effect on their everyday life. They are going to find it harder to study and learn, pay attention, be relaxed and responsive and remain active. This, in turn, can easily lead to obesity and lethargy.

WHAT NOT TO DO

The way we present food to our children can set them up for the rest of their life. Here's one example of how not to do it taken from our archive of bad eating tales.

Joanna became worried that her four-year-old daughter, Lucy, was not eating enough, so when Lucy refused to finish her meals, Joanna smacked her with a wooden spoon. Mealtimes became a battlefield between Lucy and her mum — a no-win situation.

How could Joanna have solved the problem without resorting to the wooden spoon? First, she could have asked Lucy which foods she liked and why. Then she could have invited Lucy along to help her shop for them. Maybe the meal could be eaten in a different place from time to time, perhaps a picnic in the park or on a rug taken into the garden. She could have offered Lucy a variety of different foods and let her see Mum sitting there eating all hers up. Incidentally, it's also a good idea to avoid having meals with the television on, and encourage conversation at the table. This was a perfect opportunity for her to really listen to what Lucy had to say.

We could go on for pages about this subject, but you've probably got the point by now. Diet is important for all the reasons that we have outlined in this chapter and the whole ethic of mealtimes is vital to the wellbeing of children. It is a time when the whole family can come together around the table. It is a time for talk and laughter. It is an opportunity to let your children have their say and listen to them. You can probably learn more about your child from observing them for half an hour at the dining table than you can from any other time during the day.

SEVEN TIPS FOR HAPPY MEALTIMES

1. Avoid making mealtimes a battleground.

2. Respect the fact that your child may not always be hungry.

3. Offer no other alternatives to the food on offer.

4. Offer nothing until the next scheduled mealtime.

5. Avoid snacks close to meals, and preferably not at all between meals.

6. Be calm, firm and consistent.

7. Never let your child see that it disturbs you when they are not hungry.

18

consistency in parenting

I f there is one single feature that should take precedence in the raising of children, it is that parents and other carers should present a united front. Communication is the key: parents need to be in agreement about all child-rearing and parenting practices. This may not always be easy but any difference you may have with your partner should be discussed, aired, cleared and sorted behind closed doors. Children will feel safe, secure and loved if they experience that you are together on parenting, but they are also absolute winners at that old rule of warfare — divide and conquer!

So what does this mean and how does it play itself out in real life? Parents may agree it is dangerous for two-year-old Lisa to climb up onto the high chair attached to the table as she is too heavy. Together they have decided on a rule based on safety, and the consequence for disobeying it. They have also agreed that the rule will be enforced every time and they are committed to being consistent.

Robert and Sally have decided that seven-year-old Oliver may use the Gameboy for only 30 minutes each evening. If he 'forgets', there is no Gameboy the next day.

Both parents have agreed on the rule and the consequence and have explained and discussed this with each other.

But look at this scenario . . . Robert is cooking dinner and Sally is out at a meeting. Oliver comes into the kitchen and says, 'Mum said I could play Gameboy for an extra 30 minutes tonight as it is a pupil-free day tomorrow.' Dad agrees that this is OK. Whoa! Robert, what happened to that agreement? Where is the consistency? Oliver is playing the age-old game of divide and conquer, or let's play Mum against Dad (or Dad against Mum). Once Oliver has learned to play this game and it has worked, he will try it on again, and again and again.

> *"Parents and carers need to be in agreement about all child-rearing and parenting practices."*

Think of the games your children could play with pocket money: 'Dad said I could have an extra five dollars this week.' You get the picture?

STEP-PARENTS

When it comes to step-parents, it is vital that the same rules apply. Step-parents need to be in agreement with the birth parents, who should feel 100 per cent supported by the step-parent. They will need to discuss the parenting strategies and consequences and be consistent in the same way we discussed above. There is nothing worse than a child who is not allowed to watch television on school days at home, coming back from a stay with his mum or dad and step-parent and saying, 'But *they* let me watch it during the week.' This completely undermines the authority of the primary caregiver and makes it impossible for all parties to exercise any consistent restraints on the child.

Initially it is important to build rapport with your stepchildren and create an environment of mutual respect which is non-threatening to the relationship the child has with their parent. Remember that you are not the parent and will not replace the parent. This does not, however, mean buying gifts and lollies all the time, but rather spending quality time playing, talking and listening. During this initial stage it is best to leave all parenting and behaviour modification to the biological parent.

As a step-parent, you will probably have all sorts of theories and ideas on what your partner could/should do, particularly if you do not have a child yourself. However it is important to build rapport. Eventually, as your relationship with your partner grows into permanency and a committed live-in relationship, as the step-parent you will obviously be a significant influencing factor in the child's life. Therefore you will also need to discuss any differences and views behind closed doors, and present a united and loving front to your stepchild. The time will surely come when you are home alone with your stepchild and the same guidelines apply. Be consistent. Remain in accord with your partner.

Picture this. It is 1950. Janet is a charismatic five-year-old, angelic looking with a head of blonde curls. Her stepfather, called 'Uncle Bill', has just painted the apartment. Janet finds her pencils and 'draws' on the walls, so Janet's mother, furious, tells her in no uncertain terms that Uncle Bill will deal with her when he gets home from work. Janet, being such a delightful child, meets Uncle Bill at the front door, chanting, 'I writ on the walls! I writ on the walls!' then does a record-breaking sprint down the front stairs and into the apartment where Uncle Bill's mother lives. Bill arrives, puffing and red-faced to find the rascal hiding behind Grandma, who stands protectively with outstretched arms saying 'You can't smack her, she is not your child!'

So what did Janet learn? Very effectively how to manipulate her stepdad . . . and Mum won't do anything anyway, no matter what she does.

SEPARATION AND DIVORCE

One of the most important things to remember during separation and divorce is that young children will often believe they are to blame. They may even think their behaviour caused the split. It is hard for children to understand that parents need to separate, so it is necessary to explain clearly to the child that they are loved by both parents. It is important to spend some time finding out just how your child is feeling. Encourage and allow these feelings to be expressed. Encourage them to talk about their feelings with other trusted adults. It is also necessary to demonstrate this love by giving affection and attention.

Sometimes, during separation, parents allow their own emotions and feelings of anger, resentment and disappointment to be played out on their children. Children are often bribed with expensive toys and manipulated into discussing the 'other' parent in inappropriate ways. Do not make your child feel they have to choose between the two of you. Make it easy for children to keep in contact with all relatives.

When Jack's parents separated, he was two years old. His parents had an unusual agreement: to create as stable an environment as they could by decorating his room in exactly the same way in both houses. His cot was in the same position with the same mobile hanging overhead, his toys were in the same place and the walls were even the same colour.

We have known of parents who leave the children in the one primary house and the parents rotate caring for them!

These sorts of examples may not work for everyone who finds themself in this position, but they are good examples of innovative thinking, cooperation and respecting what is best for the children.

GRANDPARENTS

Grandparents often play an important role in the lives of children. These days many are taking on the role of carers as parents return to the workforce, so it is important for parents and grandparents to establish healthy communications and mutual respect.

It is vital that grandparents respect the parents' wishes, even though their own ways of raising children may have been quite different. Children will feel safe, loved and nurtured if the ground rules are the same in both environments. A confused child is invariably an unhappy child.

When putting in place some strategies for modifying behaviours, parents need to be gentle but firm in communicating their wishes to the grandparents. They need to enlist the grandparents as allies and, as in their own relationship, need to discuss how the children should be handled well out of earshot of little ears. Of course, if you are using grandparents as free babysitters it is only reasonable that they be allowed some input.

OTHER CARERS

Caregivers have a duty of care to respect parents' wishes. It is necessary for the benefit of the child that all carers, be they family daycarers, nannies, long daycarers or preschools, form strong partnerships with the parents of the children in their care. This means the sharing and exchanging of information between parents and carers.

Looking after young children, particularly two- to four-year-olds, can be demanding and challenging just by the very essence of who they are at that stage. They are constantly on the go, running, laughing, crying, exploring, investigating everything, and often it seems that carers need to have as many arms as an octopus! Nevertheless, carers must take time to share information and really listen to parents. This can enable a much richer and more meaningful environment in which the child may grow, learn and develop.

Sasha is the mother of two-year-old William, who goes to two different family daycare mothers (mothers licensed to look after up to five children in their home). Both these women are caring, loving, professional people. However, there is a fundamental difference between the two of them: one is in accord with William's parents, and one isn't. On most days the first daycare mum sends home a communication book. The first day it described how his day had been and how he settled in. Some days she is too busy playing, comforting, sharing and caring for the children to write in the book, but she has demonstrated that she is definitely on the same wavelength. Recently Sasha gave William a yellow ice-block on a very hot day. He had an allergic reaction to the yellow food colouring, and had a bad asthma attack. When informed of this, the daycare mum was supportive and took the information on board. Now included in the communication book is the detail of anything he may have eaten during the day. This has made Sasha feel she is respected and listened to, and that her opinions about her child are valued.

On the other hand, when Sasha mentioned to the second carer that she does not give William sweet biscuits at home, the carer laughed and said, 'Wait till you have four children!' She continued to give William sweet biscuits. So while the care is still loving and professional, she is not in accord with William's parents.

Of course these actions should work both ways. If the second daycare mum says to Sasha, 'We're encouraging the children to sit at the table while they eat their food — do you do this at home?', there is an opportunity for Sasha to work with the daycare mum and support her in her endeavours to teach the children in her care to stay seated while they are eating. It's all about good communication.

19

conflict
resolution

C onflict is inevitable when two or more people come together in an enterprise, be it running local government or bringing up children. What is conflict? The dictionary definition is 'To be . . . in opposition . . . or disagree.' This very definition suggests that conflict will always be around because we are all different and often have differing ideas, thoughts, feelings and ideals. It is these differences that render us human. Reptiles, for example, all behave in the same way, but humans can make many choices in their everyday lives.

"Conflict is healthy — if handled properly."

This same principle applies to our children. They are different from us and as they grow older, they will, and should, be confident enough to express these differences. As parents we often feel we are right because we have more experience. We feel our children should listen to us because we are the parents.

We often create unnecessary conflict by trying to impose our will on an already strong-willed child. The stronger a child's spirit, the more emotionally healthy in fact that child is. It is the expression of our will and spirit that causes the conflict.

Conflict is healthy — if handled properly. However, to do this, two important aspects must be attended to. First, we must learn to know and feel when we are moving towards conflict: to know that something has triggered our 'conflict possible' button. Secondly, the desired outcome is that both parties are OK — sometimes known as win/win. It means one party has not fully surrendered or compromised, and a suitable outcome has been arrived at where both parties feel happy about themselves and the other person. It does not mean we have to agree with the other person, just be able to respect them and respect ourselves. And of course the key to all this is good communication.

WHY CONFLICT OCCURS

Conflict occurs for the following reasons.

Conditioning

This is the way we respond to stimuli on a conscious and unconscious level. We are conditioned by parents, teachers, peers, families and the media, usually at a subconscious level, through messages that reinforce existing belief systems. To protect our beliefs, we may engage in conflict as an automatic survival response. For example, we may have been conditioned as a child to believe that being tidy was good and untidy bad. So, as parents, when our little untidy one shows up, we create conflict around the tidiness issue.

Filters

Filters alter or distort the way we look at things. While we are wearing all the filters given to us by our conditioned past, we cannot see things as they are. So again we may engage in conflict to prove that our belief systems are right. Filters give us fixations, so we set out to prove them right — for example, the belief that pink and blue do not go together. When Sally comes out of her room wearing pink and blue, we will tell her to take it off, because of our filter. The reality is that anything goes with anything. Our filters tell us what our personal taste is, not what reality is.

Inflexibility

Our belief systems become locked. We bring understanding from our past and previous experiences to new situations, and tend to see things as we believe they are, not as they really are. This is related to our filters. We become unbending — perhaps saying 'no' routinely without weighing the situation up and making a decision based on the immediate facts rather than being on automatic pilot. The pink–blue clothing combination just mentioned is a perfect example — instead of automatically telling Sally to go and change, we could stop and see how important it really is. What is the worst thing that could happen if she wore pink and blue? Answer: nothing.

Therefore, is it really important enough to disrupt the relationship? Finally, are we being respectful to her? What message is she receiving when we tell her that her choice of colours is no good? We are doing little more than eroding her self-esteem and telling her either that she has a rotten colour sense or that she shouldn't think for herself.

Unstimulating environment

When people are bored they tend to become picky and dissatisfied, so are more easily riled and led into arguments. Parents need to check their contentment levels from time to time. Often we enter into conflict with our children because we are frustrated about an unrelated issue. It is also vital to ensure that our children have harmonious and interesting rooms. Some children's rooms are just so exciting to be in and others have nothing on the walls. Their rooms should be a place where they do things their way. Many parents will get shudders down their backs with this statement, but it really is important. Obviously, when children are very young, it is the parents who will organise their room, but as they start showing independence and a unique style, parents need to honour that and allow them to develop their own space in the way they would like — even if it does mean painting the walls black!

Mental anchors

Most of the passengers on the *Titanic* could have been saved had it not been assumed that the ship was unsinkable.

However, because of that belief, no safety drill had ever taken place, and there weren't enough lifeboats. As parents we become anchored to certain perceptions of reality and, sometimes, in spite of the evidence, we may persist in holding on to that mindset.

Remember, your child is special. All children are special, even when they are driving you crazy. We can use the analogy of cutting an apple here. Children are like the centre of an apple, cut horizontally you see a star — but only if recognised. If the apple is cut vertically we do not see the star.

REDUCING CONFLICT

It is a parent's responsibility to bring out the best in their children. One way of doing this is to reduce conflict and manage it when it does occur. Remember, the objective in dealing with conflict is that both parties need to be happy with the outcome and feel OK about themselves. If this can be achieved, then the conflict cannot harm the child's self-esteem and will not damage the relationship.

People deal with conflict in different ways. There are those who face it head on and deal with it. Then there are those who will avoid it at all costs. Avoiding conflict is a bit like trying to stuff too much meat into a sausage skin: eventually the sausage is going to explode. It is far better to face it and deal with it before it escalates to explosive proportions.

When it comes to facing conflict, we do need to be careful, however. Such confrontation has the power either to enhance a relationship or destroy it. Conflict can be heightened rather than solved if handled ineffectively.

Generally, people tend to handle conflict in one of two major ways — fight or flight.

Fight

- 'I'm right and you're wrong'
- Blame and punishment
- Threats
- Screaming
- Physical violence
- Refusing to listen
- Manipulation
- Sulking
- 'I'm OK and you're not'

Flight

- Sulking
- Crying
- Pretending it did not happen
- Giving in
- 'I'm wrong and you're right'
- Avoiding conflict
- Anything to maintain peace
- Allowing the other person to win
- 'I'm not OK and you are'

There are, however, some healthy options — it is not necessary to fall directly into one of these two modes of operating. When next faced with a conflict with your child, try these:

- Discuss the issue.
- Listen to each other.
- Explain your own perspective and needs.
- Find another way to solve the issues.
- Sort out the problem.
- Respect others.
- Ensure everybody is satisfied with the solution.

THE WIN/WIN PRINCIPLE

We have spoken about the win/win principle, but what exactly does it entail? Well, for a start it means considering not only what you want, but also what the other person wants. It means respecting relationships, considering what is actually fair, and, above all, knowing that for you to win does not automatically mean somebody else has to lose. In moving towards a solution you need to include as many needs as possible and consider all the options.

The benefits in using this approach with your children are as follows:

- An increase in self-esteem
- The encouragement of creativity
- The eliciting of good communication skills
- Energy and attention is focused on solving the problem, rather than fighting with one another

So here's the bottom line:

- Go for the win/win.
- Be clear about what you feel and why you feel it.
- Consider everybody's needs.
- Ask yourself how important the issue is exactly.
- Ask yourself how your child feels, and how you'd feel in their position.
- Think: How can we solve this? What else can be done?
- Focus on the desired outcome.
- Ensure everybody feels OK.

Children need to learn to deal with conflict. The children who have the most problems in life are those who are never exposed to conflict and when they encounter it, they have no idea how to deal with it, which destroys their confidence and often makes them feel like failures. Parents can teach children how to deal with conflict effectively and this should begin very early in their lives.

Here's a story about two little girls who both wanted the only orange. Their mother decided the fairest way was to cut the orange in half. Both girls were distraught and did not want that. After much screaming and crying, Mum asked the girls why they didn't want her to cut the orange. 'Because,' cried Stephanie, 'I want the juice for the recipe I am making.' 'Because,' cried Penny, 'I want the peel for my artwork!'

Now that's win/win!

20

staying safe

I t is remarkable just how many dangerous things we take for granted as adults. We often don't think twice about leaving the handle of a saucepan sticking out over the edge of the stove or changing a light globe with the electricity still switched on. However, when there are children around, we need to be a lot more careful.

For first-time parents this can be a case of discovering as you go; however, there will be fewer mishaps and less stress if some strategies have been put in place before your baby arrives. They don't stay babies for long — the speed at which they grow into toddlers and the speed with which they begin to move is amazing. One day they cannot reach the kitchen bench and the next they are up there discovering the joys of the recently boiled kettle.

That's why it is so important to put your home through a childproofing inspection every year. By taking stock and recognising the hidden dangers, your home can be a much safer place for your child. Remember also that there will be other children visiting your home, now that you have entered the magical, fun-filled world of parenthood. So while your toddler may not be interested in the knife drawer, your friend's child may well be. So you might ask, 'What can I leave out in my kitchen?' The answer is not much in the lower cupboards and drawers. All young children love playing with saucepans and plastic containers. This will afford many hours of pleasure, noise and fun! So keep these in the lower cupboards and put the more dangerous items higher up.

"It is important to put your home through a childproofing inspection every year."

Electricity is another danger point. You may not have needed outlet covers when your child was a newborn, but now that they are learning to crawl, electrical outlets can pose a serious hazard. And that's not all. Fires and burns, drowning, suffocation, choking, poisoning, falls and other injuries inside the home cause the majority of home injury deaths to children. See the Appendix for some simple tips for childproofing your home.

WATCH OUT FOR THE INTERNET

While on the subject of dangers in the home, there is another area that has recently become dangerous ground for young children and teenagers: the Internet. As more and more young children launch themselves into cyberspace, it is important that they are taught how to protect themselves from the predators they may find out there.

While we recommend that children up to the age of six or seven are far better off making up their own games and playing outdoors, we recognise that it is a fact of life nowadays that some preschoolers may have access to the Internet and learn about computers. If you are going to allow them to do this, then it is advisable to sit with them and teach them Net navigation and computer skills via educational games on appropriate websites. Children from about five years may start to visit children's websites with you, and to enjoy email correspondence with family and friends (a great way to start learning keyboard skills). On the other hand, if you would prefer your child not to start this early, don't feel that you are penalising them unduly, because we can assure you, they will catch up rapidly.

From around eight years old, children become increasingly interested in exploring the Internet, chatting and corresponding online. Some older children may begin to assert their independence and look for 'forbidden' material. They may be targeted by marketers, but increasingly they learn to recognise the difference between advertising and other material.

It helps to talk to children about commercial information and how to deal with it. While their skills and independence are increasing, making Internet exploration a family activity allows you to maintain close supervision.

Here are some valuable rules developed by the Australian Broadcasting Authority for parents, and you can find out more from the website (www.cybersmartkids.com.au).

Young ones (2–7 years)

- Check out good sites for young ones — you should be responsible for selecting the sites that children in this age group can visit.
- Very close supervision is strongly recommended.
- Select sites and set up bookmarks for very young users.
- Consider using safe zones for this age group, particularly when they start school and can do more on their own.
- Limit email correspondence to a list of friends and family you have approved.
- Use filters to limit accidental access to unsuitable material.

Kids (8–11 years)

- Be actively involved in your child's Internet use.
- Emphasise the safe behaviour tips in the following cyber rules and discuss why these are needed.
- Investigate any chat rooms or online clubs your child wants to join, to make sure they are legitimate.
- Consider using filters to block access to Internet Relay Chat (IRC) and newsgroups.
- Discuss use of good cyber manners (Netiquette), just as you do for the real world.
- Put the computer in a public area of the home, to help keep an eye on what's going on.
- Use search engines designed for children.

Cyber rules

Here is an important set of rules you may want to copy and pin up next to your child's or the family's computer:

1. Ask your parents or carer before you give anyone on the Internet your name or address or any other personal details. This includes the name of your school, your photo or any personal information about your friends or family.
2. Meeting people online might be fun, but remember the people you meet online may not be who they say they are. Someone claiming to be a 12-year-old girl may be a 40-year-old man.
3. If you want to meet someone you have so far only met online, ask a parent or another adult to go with you. And always meet in a popular public place, preferably during the day.
4. Keep your password a secret, never give it to anyone (even your best friend).
5. If someone writes something rude or something that makes you feel uncomfortable in chat or email, leave the chat room and don't respond to the email.
6. Tell your parent or another adult you trust if you see upsetting language, nasty pictures or something scary on the Internet.
7. Always ask a parent or adult before you fill out any forms, or give out money or credit card details.
8. Don't accept any offers that seem too good to be true — they probably are.

SAFETY OUTSIDE THE HOME

Then there's the problem of safety *outside* the home as your child grows older. There is a marvellous program in Australia known as the Protective Behaviours Program. It was brought into Australia from the USA by the Victorian police to replace the Stranger Danger Program and is now used in all states. It recognises (sadly) that many children are harmed by their own families and those close to them.

We don't want to be alarmist, but if this program is used both in the home and at school it will help to develop confident children with high self-esteem. It sets children up with particular skills and tools to deal with any difficult situation they may come across.

The problem may be teasing in the classroom or bullying in the playground. It may be what to do if you are five years old and have forgotten lunch. Ultimately it equips children to be confident, self-assured and assertive, and able to deal with conflict or difficult situations in the home and, later on, as adults in the workplace.

The theme as it is taught to the younger children is 'We all have the right to feel safe' and 'When I feel scared I can find someone to talk to.'

This program then begins to help children become aware of their feelings and emotions and discover how they experience these feelings in the body. Games are played such as running fast on the spot, then noticing how fast their heart is beating. Discussions, which can also help develop confident children with self-esteem, are based on what may happen inside your body when you are excited or scared. The children are then asked about what makes them scared. Most very young children proudly reply, 'nothing'. So then the program often has to introduce role models.

An example might be feeling scared when climbing up a ladder — leading to clammy hands and a tummy that feels like a washing machine. It is stressed that everyone is different. Children then get the idea and come up with all sorts of explanations, such as 'I get butterflies in my tummy', and everyone has a good laugh imagining what it would look like to have real butterflies in their tummies. The next time this is discussed, young children are more likely to suggest things that make them feel scared.

Stories are also frequently used to illustrate fear, so when, for example, teddy gets left outside in the dark alone, you may say at the end of the story, 'How do you think the teddy felt being left outside?' Children will then come up with 'scared, frightened and lonely'. After another story, when asked, 'How did Johnny feel when his brother trod on his caterpillar?', they may reply 'angry or annoyed'.

The children are then asked to liken their bodies to an ambulance with the red light and the siren. They are warning signs and similarly the body has 'early warning signs', including sweaty palms, racing heart, wobbly legs, and hairs standing up on the back of neck. Children learn to describe these.

The program is based on the premise that parents cannot be with their children all hours of the day — the children are equipped to know when they are feeling scared (experiencing those early warning signs) and ultimately in an uncomfortable or dangerous situation.

The second part of this theme is 'When I feel scared I can find someone to talk to.' So next they learn about networking.

This part sets up the children from as young as three years of age with a network hand. A hand is drawn and on it the child writes the names of various adults with whom they feel safe and whom they can seek out if they have a problem. Family members are all written on the thumb, and other adults on the fingers.

For this activity you can also draw a train with carriages for very young children, though we like the idea of the hand because your hand is always with you! The child must think up the names. It is not about who *you* think might be suitable. Quite often they choose the most unexpected people.

Songs and games can also be used to reinforce the themes, particularly asking someone for help and persisting until someone listens to you. Puppets can be used to demonstrate this. For example, Koala Kim has to tell five different animals her problem until finally someone really listens to her and helps to solve the problem. Role modelling is also good. Allow your child to see you call your sister to talk and receive comfort and advice when you are worried or upset. Talk about your own network hand.

From a very early age you can teach the child to say, 'Stop it, I don't like it.' Often even friendly tickling by Mum or Dad changes from feeling good to uncomfortable. So empower your child to use these words.

Teach your children your phone number or set them up with phone cards so they know you are always available should they need you.

TEACHING CHILDREN TO THINK FOR THEMSELVES

Brainstorming skills are also another vital part of this empowering program. These skills can be taught every day in many ways. When brainstorming, remember there are no incorrect answers, just allow the ideas to flow and then discuss or discount after the brainstorming session has finished. A brainstorming session may start like this: 'Imagine Harry has arrived home from school one day and the house is locked. What could he do?'

So you start to brainstorm ideas and actually write them down. Some of the ideas of what Harry could do are:

- Go next door.
- Sit and wait till Mum or Dad gets home from work.
- Break a window to get in.
- Burn the house down.
- Go back to school.

So we write down all the ideas, then discuss them. Ask what would happen if, for example, you burnt the house down? Well, replies the seven-year-old Tom, the fire-engine would come with a big ladder! Obviously not a very good idea, but nevertheless, an idea. As we continue the discussion the child sees for themself the best solution. Having practised and developed this skill, they will quickly brainstorm and sort out the ideas to come up with an excellent solution if they find themself in a difficult situation.

You can also use this technique with day-to-day fun activities. For example, brainstorm ideas for Grandpa's birthday present, food to take on the picnic, what to take to the beach, where to go for a holiday, what to have for dinner tonight. During these sessions it is important to encourage children to express what they like as well as what they do not like. This also helps develop confident children with high self-esteem.

This in no way covers the entire program, but gives an overview of what you can expect. We would recommend parents and teachers make enquiries at their state branch of the Protective Behaviours Consultancy Group and obtain literature and books for their home and school.

Safety out of doors

Lastly, here are some ways in which you can make life safer for your child out of doors:

- Make a list with your children of their neighbourhood boundaries, choosing significant landmarks.
- Interact regularly with your neighbours. Tell your children whose homes they are allowed to visit.
- Don't drop your children off alone at malls, movie theatres, video arcades or parks. Teach your children that

adults should not approach children for help or
directions. Tell your children that if they are approached
by an adult, they should stay alert because this may be a
'trick'.

- Never leave children unattended in a car.
- Children should never hitchhike or approach a car when
  they don't know and trust the driver.
- Children should never go anywhere with anyone without
  having your permission first.

SAFETY AT SCHOOL

Be careful when you put your child's name on
clothing, backpacks, lunch boxes or bicycle licence
plates. If a child's name is visible, it may put them on
a first-name basis with an abductor.

Walk the route to and from school with your
children, pointing out landmarks and safe places
to go if they're being followed or need help. Make a
map with your children showing acceptable routes
to school, using main roads and avoiding shortcuts
or isolated areas. If your children take a bus, visit
the bus stop with them and make sure they know
which bus to take.

postscript

I f you have read this far, your notion of parenthood will
have been confirmed — bringing up a child is a constantly
puzzling undertaking with as many pitfalls as a Himalayan
mountain pass. It is important not to be too uptight about this,
though. Most parents don't master it all until their ninth or
tenth child, and the majority don't get that far!

SUMMING IT ALL UP

So, in conclusion, let's sum up some of the more salient
features of the book.

The workings of the brain

How this organ governs a child's behaviour is of paramount
importance. Understand which part of the brain your child is
working in and half the battle's already won.

Parental attitudes and beliefs

Just because your mother did things her way, and her mother
before her, doesn't make them right. Take yourself off automatic

pilot and adapt your own ways of child-rearing. If it feels right, it probably is!

Make your child feel special
Every child needs to feel loved and wanted. Every child is unique and that uniqueness needs to be recognised, whether you have one child or ten. Make time for your children.

Think before you speak
It's easy to give your children 'don't exist' messages without meaning to. 'Grow up', 'Don't be such a nuisance'. . . all phrases that slip out easily but carry devastating messages for young, immature minds.

Listen to what your children are saying
Active listening is one of the hardest of all skills to learn, especially in a busy world. Nevertheless, it is important that you show your child you are listening to — and taking in — what they are trying to tell you. Only when they feel that you are listening will they feel secure.

Never assume your child understands
If there is only one lesson you take home from reading his book, let this be it. Children are capable of reacting in exactly the same way as Japanese taxi drivers do to foreign tourists. They nod and say 'yes' but haven't understood a word! If you want to make sure that your child has understood what you

have just told them, make them repeat it back to you. And remember, only ask a child to do one thing at a time. That's about as much as a young child can cope with.

Remember the importance of play and free time

Playing is how children learn at an early age. Filling up their days with busy-ness is generally counter-productive. Keep TV watching and computer games to a minimum. Make them get out and about.

Healthy diets for healthy children

This hardly needs elaboration. But the secret to giving your child a healthy diet is to have one yourself. Children are the world's greatest mimics and you will never get them to eat a salad sandwich while you're chomping into a hamburger. Watch out for the direct and indirect effects that some foodstuffs can have on children. Make a list and stick it on your fridge.

Agree on your parenting style and stick to it

There's nothing more confusing for a child than to have five different sets of rules. Parents, grandparents, step-parents, carers, teachers — get together and agree on how the child is going to be brought up. Don't ever allow anyone to undermine your authority. You're the parent. You're in charge.

Good luck!

NOTES

1. 'This Be the Verse', Philip Larkin, *The Collected Poems of Philip Larkin* (The Marvell Press, Faber & Faber, London, 1988).

2. The Interactive Bible, California, USA (www.bible.ca).

3. *The Secret Life of the Unborn Child*, Dr Thomas Verny (Sphere Books, London, 1982).

4. *Male–Female Brain Differences*, Dr Daniel Amen, the Amen Clinics Inc (www.BrainPlace.com).

5. *Brain Gym*, Paul and Gail Dennison (Edu-Kinesthetics Inc, California, 1986).

6. The diagnostic Inventory of Basic Skills was developed by American educator Albert Brigance in 1981 and assesses basic readiness and academic skills in key subject areas from kindergarten to sixth-grade level.

7. *Prenatal and Perinatal Psychology and Medicine: A Comprehensive Survey of Research and Practice*, Peter Fedor-Freybergh and Vanessa Vogel (eds) (Mattes Verlag, Heidelberg, 1988).

8. *The Prophet*, Kahlil Gibran (Alfred A. Knopf, New York, 1923).

9. *Antisocial Behavior: Personality Disorders from Hostility to Homicide*, Benjamin B. Wolman (Prometheus Books, New York, 1999).

10. 'Language and Reading Outcomes to Age 9 in Late-talking Toddlers', Leslie Rescorla, PhD, in *Journal of Speech, Language & Hearing Research*, vol. 45.

11. *The Creative Brain*, Ned Herrmann (Brain Books, North Carolina, USA, 1993).

12. *Discipline Without Tears*, R. Dreikurs, P. Cassel and P. Hawthorn (Wiley, New York, 1972).

13. *The Importance of Play in Your Pre-Schooler's Life*, Thomas Armstrong PhD, ParentsPlace.com, The Parenting Resource Centre on the Web, 1995.

14. *Einstein Never Used Flash Cards*, Dr Kathy Hirsh-Pasek (Rodale Press, New York, 2003).

15. Article by Dr Alan Greene on DrGreene.com: *Caring for the Next Generation*, Greene Ink Inc, 2003.

16. Cardiff University, South Wales, Regeneration Unit: research findings, December 2003.

appendix

SIMPLE TIPS FOR CHILDPROOFING YOUR HOME

Safety, not convenience, comes first

Busy parents and people without children are more likely to store household items with convenience, rather than safety, as the top priority. Curious kids can be very determined, so lock all potentially harmful products out of their reach.

Examine everything in the home from the vantage point of a young child

Get down on the floor on your hands and knees and explore the home the way a curious young child might. You may feel silly, but taking this precaution is far better than any tragic alternative for your child or loved one.

Cover every room in the home

During your inspection, ask yourself what looks tempting. What is within reach? Look for potential dangers between the

270

floor and about 1 metre above the floor. Also, check floors and carpets for buried dangers such as pins or coins. Remove or correct any potential hazards.

Set hot water heaters no higher than 48° Celsius

A lower water temperature will reduce the chance of scald burns. It takes just three seconds for a child to sustain a third-degree burn, requiring hospitalisation and skin grafts, from water at 60° Celsius.

Memorise the Poisons Information Centre national phone number: 13 11 26

In the event of a poisoning, Poisons Information staff are available at this hotline 24 hours a day, seven days a week, from anywhere in Australia.

Check the house for fire hazards

Look for obvious fire hazards such as frayed electrical wires or flammable materials near heat sources such as space heaters. Never run electrical cords under rugs. Make sure your home, and any home your child visits, has working smoke alarms in every sleeping area and on every level. Make sure to check the batteries on each alarm monthly and replace batteries annually if your alarms are not wired in.

Use safety gates

Stairs are particularly dangerous, and falls from stairs tend to result in more severe injuries. Use safety gates at both the top and bottom of stairs to keep infants and toddlers out of harm's way.

Post emergency numbers by every telephone

In addition to the Poisons Information Centre, emergency numbers should include 000, the doctor, the local police station, medical services and a neighbour.

Keep first aid supplies on hand

Make sure babysitters know where to find the supplies in your home and how to respond in an emergency.

Although it is impossible to remove all of the dangers from your child's environment, with the proper precautions, your home can still be their haven.

Some practical suggestions

In addition to these major precautions, here are some other practical suggestions for making your home safer:

- Pack away all valuable and breakable ornaments.
- Place all cleaning materials and garden chemicals out of the reach of any child.

- Place knives out of reach of any child.
- Place glass and crockery in high cupboards.
- Purchase childproof locks for kitchen cupboards and the fridge.
- Keep hot coffee and tea out of reach of any child.
- Have shatterproof glass on sliding doors and affix stickers at child height.
- Place all medication in a locked cupboard out of the reach of children.
- Turn saucepan handles inwards.
- Consider barricading the kitchen from toddlers.
- Dispose of all medications thoughtfully once they are no longer required.

If you attend to these things you will be providing a safe environment where your young child can explore and experiment. Your life will be less stressful and you will not have to be following your child around saying, 'Don't touch this and don't touch that!'

INDEX

Index

Index

Index

Index